# Lecture Notes in Business Information Processing 343

Wei Wang

# Integrating Business Process Models and Rules

## Empirical Evidence and Decision Framework

Wei Wang ⓘ
School of Information Technology
and Electrical Engineering
University of Queensland
Brisbane, QLD, Australia

This book is a revised version of the PhD dissertation written by the author at the School of Information Technology and Electrical Engineering of the University of Queensland, Australia.

ISSN 1865-1348           ISSN 1865-1356  (electronic)
Lecture Notes in Business Information Processing
ISBN 978-3-030-11808-2        ISBN 978-3-030-11809-9  (eBook)
https://doi.org/10.1007/978-3-030-11809-9

Library of Congress Control Number: 2018967684

This Springer imprint is published by the registered company Springer Nature Switzerland AG
The registered company address is: Gewerbestrasse 11, 6330 Cham, Switzerland

To my beloved parents and relatives
谨以此书献给我亲爱的父母和亲人们

# Preface

This book encompasses a revised version of the PhD dissertation written by the author, at the School of Information Technology and Electrical Engineering of the University of Queensland (Australia). In 2018, the PhD dissertation won the "CAiSE PhD Award," granted to outstanding PhD theses in the field of information systems engineering.

Over the past two decades, the need to model business rules in an integrated manner with business process models has been argued theoretically as well as validated empirically, and a variety of integration methods have been developed. However, several open research questions remained.

First, while researchers have argued that integrated modelling of business process models and business rules can improve user understanding of business processes, this proposition has neither been theoretically analyzed nor empirically evaluated. Second, there are situations in which a business rule is better modelled independently of a business process model, but also situations in which it is more appropriate to integrate the rule with a business process model. An important aspect of integrated modelling is the understanding of such situations and how they influence business rule representation.

To address these open questions, the research has the following three objectives: (1) theoretically analyze and empirically evaluate if and when business rule integration can improve business process model understanding, (2) identify and evaluate factors that will influence the decision of whether or not a business rule should be integrated with a business process model, and (3) develop a decision framework that guides modellers on whether or not, and if so how, to integrate a business rule with a business process model. Accordingly, three studies were carried out to fulfill each of these objectives.

The first study is an experiment empirically evaluating whether business rule integration can improve business process model understanding. This study used an experiment investigating the effect of process model understanding of a specific rule integration approach, rule linking, which uses graphical links to connect process model symbols with rules. We used traditional measurements to test the understanding performance and used neurophysiological measurements to observe the cognitive load and other cognitive behaviors. The study results showed that rule integration via rule linking can improve the understanding of process models, thus empirically evaluated the arguments of rule integration introduced in Chapters 1 and 2, and provided motivation for the second study.

The second study is an exploratory study identifying and evaluating factors that influence the decision of whether or not a business rule should be integrated with a business process model. In Study 2, a systematic process of identification of factors that are thought to influence the integration decision was conducted. A systematic literature review was conducted to identify these factors, resulting in 12 factors being identified.

The evaluation, via a survey with experts, resulted in the identification of four factors that affect the integration decision.

The third study follows a design science research to develop a decision framework that guides modellers on whether to integrate a business rule with a business process model. The decision framework is designed based on the synthesis of literature and insights from Study 1 and Study 2.

This book combines multiple research methods, experiment, survey, and design science, as well as traditional measurements and neurophysiological techniques that can capture a variety of cognitive behaviors in human information processing, providing more solid and comprehended research findings. While the focus of the book is the modelling of process models and rules, the methods and techniques used in this book can also be adopted and applied to broader conceptual modelling research incorporating a variety of notations (e.g., UML, ER diagrams) or ontologies.

November 2018                                                                                      Wei Wang

# Acknowledgments

First I would like to express my gratitude to my advisors, Professor Shazia Sadiq and Professor Marta Indulska. They are the best advisors I have ever met. The deeper I go in the academic world, the more I realize how outstanding, dedicated, and inspiring they are as advisors. They expanded my field of vision, taught me how to doubt carefully, how to think critically, how to write logically, and how to research independently. I must thank them for all their elaborate and generous guidance and help during the years of my PhD. This book would not have been possible without them. I owe many thanks to their insightful advice and ongoing support for my academic career.

I would like to express my gratitude to my parents for their care and support over the past 31 years. I feel so honored and proud to have them as my parents. I have to thank my parents for everything they have given to me. I know how much they sacrificed for me. Words cannot describe how important they are to me. They are the best parents in the world, and I owe my success to them. Also, I would like to thank all the members of my extended family. They always gave me the most love, made me feel special, and encouraged me all along the way.

I would like to thank Professor Barbara Weber. She hosted me during my visit to the Technical University of Denmark and gave me valuable suggestions and experience in experiment design and the use of a neurophysiological device, which made the research a very successful one and published in BPM 2017. I would like to thank Professor Selmin Nurcan for her precious advice as a member of my confirmation committee and my final thesis review committee, and for her and the CAiSE committee awarding me the CAiSE PhD Thesis Award.

Further, I would like to express my sincere appreciation to all members in the Data Knowledge and Engineering Group at the School of Information Technology and Electrical Engineering and in the Business Information System Cluster at UQ Business School. They gave me insightful input on my research, especially Professor Xiaofang Zhou, Professor Xue Li, Associate Professor Helen Huang, Dr. Hongzhi Yin, Professor Ron Weber, Professor Andrew Burton-Jones, and Dr. Dongming Xu. I also would like to thank my fellow PhD students. I am so lucky that I could learn from and work with so many talented people: Henry Roa Marin, Vimukthi Jayawardene, Faisal Khan, Feliks Prasepta Sejahtera, Ruojing Zhang, Tina Tianwa Chen, Dongfang Yang, Xufei Li, Hongyun Cai, Tony Weitong Chen, Wen Hua, Xingzhong Du, Weiqing Wang, Jiewei Cao, Peng Wang, Qingzhe Zhang, Han Su, Fang Liu, and Yunfei Shi.

Without a successful foundation of bachelor and master studies, it is hardly possible to become successful in pursuit of a PhD. Thus I would like to thank all the teachers and student fellows who helped me over my earlier study years. Thanks to my advisor Professor Youhui Zhang for supervising and guiding me during my study at Tsinghua University. Thanks to Professor Jun Yao, Professor Yasuhiko Nakashima, Associate Professor Takashi Nakada for hosting me at NAIST during my visits in 2012 and 2013.

Thanks also to Yanhua Li, Gelin Su, and Ziqiang Qian for teaching me a lot about research. Thanks to Mrs. Jinping Hou for pulling me back in when I was disappointed about the future and lost interest in studying. Thanks to Professor Weiqing Dong, Professor Xiaoshe Dong, Professor Weiguo Wu, Professor Qingping Zhao, Professor Boqin Feng, for providing me with a solid foundation of computer science skills. Thanks to Zhe Li, Ertong Zhang, Yunning Qin, Jincheng Li, Pei Chen, Xiping Kou, Adam Wenqiang Shao, Jia Lu, Long Zhao, Kang Liu — together with them I always had the best study environment with the right balance of competition and help.

Finally, I would also like to express my gratitude to the following organizations:

The CAiSE Committee, for awarding me the prestigious CAiSE PhD Award. Receiving this award was an honor and provided me with encouragement to continue with a research career.

The China Scholarship Council, for its financial assistance in the form of a State Scholarship for the three and a half years of my PhD candidature.

The University of Queensland Graduate School and School of Information Technology and Electrical Engineering, for their financial support in the form of the GSITA award and the scholarships.

# Contents

1 Introduction............................................................. 1
   1.1 Overview......................................................... 1
   1.2 Background....................................................... 2
   1.3 Aim and Objectives.............................................. 4
   1.4 Outline of the Book ............................................. 7

2 Literature Review...................................................... 9
   2.1 Overview......................................................... 9
   2.2 Business Process Models......................................... 9
   2.3 Business Process Understanding................................ 14
   2.4 Business Rules.................................................. 18
   2.5 Business Process Model and Business Rule Integration .......... 22
   2.6 Integration Approaches ......................................... 24
   2.7 Chapter Summary............................................... 28

3 Methodology........................................................... 29
   3.1 Research Method of Study 1 – Experiment .................... 30
   3.2 Research Method of Study 2 – Systematic Literature Review
      and Survey.................................................... 31
   3.3 Research Method of Study 3 – Design Science................. 32
   3.4 Chapter Summary............................................... 33

4 Rule Integration and Model Understanding: A Theoretical Underpinning... 34
   4.1 Overview......................................................... 34
   4.2 Related Theories................................................. 34
   4.3 Process Models and Rules Understanding ..................... 38
   4.4 Chapter Summary............................................... 41

5 The Effect of Rule Linking on Business Process Model Understanding.... 42
   5.1 Overview......................................................... 42
   5.2 Hypotheses Development........................................ 42
   5.3 Approach........................................................ 44
   5.4 Result Analysis................................................. 50
   5.5 Chapter Summary............................................... 59

6 Identification of Factors Affecting Business Process and Business
Rule Integration ......................................................... 60
   6.1 Overview......................................................... 60
   6.2 Approach........................................................ 60
   6.3 Business Rule Modelling Factors .............................. 63
   6.4 Empirical Validation of Factors .............................. 66

6.5  Business Rule Embedding Guidelines . . . . . . . . . . . . . . . . . . . . . .      68
6.6  Chapter Summary . . . . . . . . . . . . . . . . . . . . . . . . . . . . . . . . . . . . .      72

7 A Business Rule Modelling Decision Framework . . . . . . . . . . . . . . . . .      73
7.1  Overview . . . . . . . . . . . . . . . . . . . . . . . . . . . . . . . . . . . . . . . . . . .      73
7.2  Problem Identification and Definition of Objectives . . . . . . . . . . . .      74
7.3  The Design and Development of the Decision Framework . . . . . . . .      75
7.4  The Decision Framework Demonstration . . . . . . . . . . . . . . . . . . . .      87
7.5  The Decision Framework Evaluation . . . . . . . . . . . . . . . . . . . . . . .      90
7.6  Chapter Summary . . . . . . . . . . . . . . . . . . . . . . . . . . . . . . . . . . . . .      93

8 Conclusion . . . . . . . . . . . . . . . . . . . . . . . . . . . . . . . . . . . . . . . . . . . . .      94
8.1  Overview . . . . . . . . . . . . . . . . . . . . . . . . . . . . . . . . . . . . . . . . . . .      94
8.2  Summary of Contributions . . . . . . . . . . . . . . . . . . . . . . . . . . . . . .      94
8.3  Research Limitations and Future Work . . . . . . . . . . . . . . . . . . . . .      97

Appendix A: Online Survey . . . . . . . . . . . . . . . . . . . . . . . . . . . . . . . . . . .      101
Appendix B: Experiment Materials . . . . . . . . . . . . . . . . . . . . . . . . . . . . .      115

References . . . . . . . . . . . . . . . . . . . . . . . . . . . . . . . . . . . . . . . . . . . . . . . .      119

# Chapter 1
# Introduction

## 1.1 Overview

Enterprise information, such as policies and procedures, enterprise data, enterprise social networks, and emails, to name a few, all reside in different information systems. This situation results in information silos, which in turn lead to the increased cost of information integration and reduced capacity for exploiting synergies within the organization. In fact, information silos in organizational information systems can result in inefficiency of information retrieval, redundancy and conflicts between information assets of the company, leading to duplication of efforts and job roles, as well as an incomplete understanding of the organization.

A prominent case of information silos can be found in business process management systems and business rule management systems. In the Business Process Management (BPM) life cycle, the success of business process (re)design, analysis, and simulation are all underpinned by the assumption that business activities are well understood. This understanding is extracted from graphical process models, which mainly focus on the temporal or logical relationships between business activities, as well as business rules, which are the constraints and mandates that control the behaviour of the process and business activities. Both business processes and business rules focus on creating a representation of the organization's policies and practices. They are complementary modelling approaches as they address distinct aspects of organizational practices. The conceptual and pragmatic overlap between business process models and business rules indicates a need to model the two related aspects together.

Over the past two decades, the need to model business rules in an integrated manner with business processes has been argued theoretically as well as validated empirically, and a variety of integration methods have been developed. However, the following questions have not yet been answered by current research.

First, while researchers have argued that integrated modelling of business process models and business rules can improve the understanding of business processes, this proposition has neither been theoretically analysed nor empirically

© Springer Nature Switzerland AG 2019
W. Wang, *Integrating Business Process Models and Rules*, LNBIP 343,
https://doi.org/10.1007/978-3-030-11809-9_1

evaluated. Second, there are situations in which a business rule is better modelled independently of a business process model, but also situations in which it is more appropriate to integrate the rule with a business process model. An analysis of these situations has not been undertaken and thus the ability of make informed decisions on modelling approaches is also compromised.

## 1.2   Background

A business process is a structured collection of activities that accomplishes a specific goal that creates value for an organization [1]. A business process model is a graphical representation of a business process, defining the ways in which operations are carried out thus to accomplish the specific objectives of an organization. The control flow, i.e. the sequence of activities in a business process model, is an essential part of organizational internal control, and business process models play a key role in the management of information systems. A business process model is used to design a business process. While making a process model, a modeller views the process from various perspectives, and designs the process according to requirements. Stakeholders use a process model to structure, discuss, and share an understanding of business practice among one another. The process models enable users to "play out" different scenarios and thus enable the designer to make modifications and justifications according to the feedback. Model based performance simulation can be used to understand the factors influencing response time, service level and other performance indicators. Model based compliance checking ensures that designed practices will be in compliance with regulations and procedures.

The modelling of business processes also involves business rules, which specify constraints, obligations, permissions, restrictions, necessities, possibilities, and prohibitions [2]. Business process models and business rules focus on different aspects of an organization's practices. Business process models focus on the activities and steps that accomplish a specific objective, and business rules limit the choice of approaches toward achieving the objective, but does not suggest a specific sequence of steps [3]. Although business process models and business rules focus on different aspects of organization's practices, they are both essential parts of organizational internal control that assures the achievement of an organization's objectives in operational effectiveness and efficiency, and compliance with laws, regulations and policies. Business rules typically fall into two categories: Rules that describe relationships and constraints among data elements (structural business rules), and rules that describe the governing principles of process execution, such as execution pathways and user privileges (behavioural business rules) [4]. The former kind can be represented in data models, while the latter kind affects activities in process models. In this research, we focus on behavioural business rules.

Business process modelling and business rule modelling both focus on creating a representation of the organization's practices (current or future). They are complementary modelling approaches as they address distinct aspects of organizational practices. The conceptual and pragmatic overlap between business process models and business rules indicates a need to model the two related aspects together [5].

While process models can incorporate complex business rules, in practice, the support for representation of business rules in process modelling notations is limited [6]. Often, organizations represent such rules in natural language (or in one of the main business rule modelling languages – e.g. [7, 8]). Anecdotal evidence suggests that organizations also store such representations in separate text documents, spreadsheets, or disconnected business rule repositories [8].

While all graphical process models generally integrate some rules (e.g. control flow of the process), business rules can be represented in an integrated manner or in a separated manner. When represented in an integrated manner, they are shown graphically in a process model, either as text annotations, as graphical links to external rules, or diagrammatically using the native notation of the graphical model. When modelled in a separated manner, they are captured in separate documents or rule engines, and the relations and connections of business process models and the rules are not explicitly represented in the process models. Traditionally, business rules, other than control flow, are modelled in a separated manner [8].

It is ideal to build in as many controls as possible in process models, since these controls, being automatic, will always be exercised since they are built into the design of the business system software. However, in practice, for reasons such as lack of business domain knowledge, difficulties in designing, the representation capacity of modelling languages, the incapability of tools and systems to support the representation of controls, the cost of software modification, and the need of flexible processes, some internal controls considered to be necessary are often not built into business process models. Instead, they are documented in business rules, which are separated from process models, and cannot work efficiently with process models to assure the operations in an organization are correct, effective, efficient, and compliance with laws, regulations and policies. Such separation of the graphical process model and relevant business rules can hinder the development of a shared understanding of a process, effective communication, process improvement, decision-making, etc., and can introduce risks of noncompliant process execution. When separation of the business process model and a set of corresponding business rules occurs, it is easy for model users to be unaware of the corresponding rules when interacting with a business process model. This situation gives rise to a risk of users inadvertently breaching required standards of operation or making ill-informed decisions. Even if the users are aware of the separate sources of information relevant to the business process of interest, they need to search for and locate the rules, interpret the relevance between each rule and a corresponding part of the process model, and, finally, they need to mentally integrate this information to form a holistic mental representation of the business process. This situation could result in different stakeholders, such as process designers, information systems developers, or process participants, having inconsistent or even conflicting understandings of the same process.

Researchers argue that the integration of business rules with business process models can achieve better process model understanding and communication [9, 10], and improved governance, risk management and control [11, 12]. At the same time, however, researchers have identified a general lack of capability and guidance among process modelling languages to adequately represent business rules [13]. For example, Green and Rosemann [14] identified limitations with respect to modelling business rules in their investigations of all five views of Architecture of Integrated Information Systems (ARIS), a popular enterprise architecture framework.

Over the past two decades the need to model business rules in an integrated manner with business processes has been argued theoretically [5, 15] as well as validated empirically [16, 17], and a variety of integration methods [11, 15, 18–23] have been developed during this time. Although the benefits and methods of integrated business rule modelling have been well studied, there is a lack of guidance outlining the circumstances under which business rules should be integrated in a business process model, yet such a decision is not a straightforward one. The answer to this rule modelling question is affected by the representational capacity of modelling languages used, the support of systems used, and the characteristics of each specific rule and process model such as if the rule updates frequently, if the rule regulates several processes, if the rule is currently well enhanced in the organization operations, etc. There are situations under which it may be more appropriate to integrate a business rule with a business process model, and situations under which a business rule is better modelled separately from a business process model. For example, while integrating business rules with the use of text annotations can provide more information to the user, such additional information increases the total number of symbols and text in the model, thus increasing the model's complexity. This increased complexity results in higher levels of difficulty in interpreting the model as a whole. Such integration may also lower business rule reuse and may make rule maintenance and update more difficult. Zur Muehlen et al. [8] were the first to argue the need for an rule integration guideline, and listed five factors (rule change frequency, implementation responsibility, understanding of implications, source of change, and scope) that could affect the decision of whether a business rule should be integrated with a process model or should be modelled separated. However, without proper evaluation, the validity of each factor cannot be fully established. Investigation and validation of each factor's decision-influence on the representation of a business rule is also needed, and a decision framework that can guide modellers to make informed decision on whether or not to integrate a business rule with a process model.

## 1.3   Aim and Objectives

The aim of this thesis is to develop a decision framework that guides modellers on whether or not to integrate a business rule with a business process model. Two questions need to be answered as prerequisites before the development of the decision framework.

First, while researchers have argued that integrated modelling can improve the understanding of business processes, this proposition has not been empirically evaluated. Current body of knowledge lacks the knowledge that if such integration can improve understanding, why such integration can improve understanding, and which aspect of understanding can such integration improves (understanding accuracy, understanding time efficiency, and the cost of mental effort in understanding). Only when we can answer these questions, we can have a deep understanding of rule integration, thus develop modelling languages and methods which can further improve the modelling of processes and rules. On the other hand, if the proposition that rule integration can improve process model understanding cannot be proven to be true, the intended decision to integrate business rules with business process models will lose its motivation. If the proposition is proven to be true, then we can go to the next question, which is to decide whether or not we should integrate a business rule with a business process model. Thus, we have our first objective:

Objective 1: Theoretically analyse and empirically evaluate whether business rule integration can improve business process model understanding.

Second, we argue, along the lines of [8], that there are situations under which a business rule is better modelled independently of a business process model, and also situations under which it is more appropriate to integrate the rule with a business process model. It follows then, that an important aspect of integrated modelling is the understanding of such situations and how they influence business rule representation. While the decision in regards to how a rule should be modelled is not a straightforward one, little guidance exists that can help modellers make such a decision. This shortcoming results in fragmented and inconsistent business process and rule models. Thus, we have our second objective:

Objective 2: Identify and evaluate factors that will influence the decision as to whether or not a business rule should be integrated with a business process model.

Finally, only after we have a conclusive, indicative answer of whether integrating business rules and business process models can improve business process model understanding, and only after we have clarified what the factors are that affect the decision as to whether or not a business rule should be integrated with a business process model, and clarified what the effects of such factors on the decision are, can we start to develop the decision framework:

Objective 3: Develop a decision framework that guides modellers on whether or not to integrate a business rule with a business process model towards achieving the benefits of integrated modelling, based on the research results from Objective 1 and Objective 2.

Accordingly, we carried out three studies to fulfil each of these objectives. We briefly introduce each of the studies here, and explain the research method we chose for each study in Chap. 3.

Study 1: An experiment empirically evaluating if business rule integration can improve business process model understanding. This study used an experiment investigating the effect of process model understanding of a specific rule integration approach, rule linking, which uses graphical links to connect process model symbols with rules. We used a cross-group experiment design with student groups, giving two groups the same process models and rules, but different rule representations. In one group, the rules are linked to process models while separated in the other group. We used comprehension questions to test the understanding accuracy and used an eye-tracker to measure the understanding efficiency. The study results showed that rule integration via rule linking can improve the understanding of process models, thus empirically evaluated the arguments of rule integration introduced in Chaps. 1 and 2, and motivated Study 2. The detailed introduction of Study 1 is in Chaps. 4 and 5.

Study 2: An exploratory study identifying and evaluating factors that will influence the decision of whether or not a business rule should be integrated with a business process model. In Study 2, we carried out a systematic process of identification of factors that are thought to influence the decision about whether or not to model business rules in an integrated manner. To identify these factors, a systematic literature review was conducted based on a comprehensive set of well-regarded Information Systems and Computer Science journals and conferences and twelve factors were identified. An online survey was carried out with the participation of the authors of the papers that were the sources for the factor identification to validate the identified factors, and to evaluate their relative importance and effects on the decision as to whether a business rule should be integrated with a process model. The evaluation resulted in four important factors that affecting the decision. The detailed introduction of Study 2 is in Chap. 6.

Study 3: Design science research, developing a decision framework that guides modellers on whether or not to integrate a business rule with a business process model. The decision framework is designed based on knowledge in literature and knowledge built in Study 1 and Study 2, and consists of 3 components. The inputs, the outputs, and the model. The inputs include a process model repository, a rule repository, and the modeller's inputs of the characteristics of a rule such as the need of accessibility, agility, change frequency, the need of reusability, etc. The modeller's knowledge about the rule, the relevant process models, the modelling languages and systems being used, and other organizational settings are essential for the modeller to measure the characteristics of a rule. The outputs of the decision framework are the four possible solutions of how to model a business rule, including (1) model the rule separately, (2) link the rule with related process models, (3) diagrammatically embed the rule, or (4) embed the rule as texts. The model part of the decision framework follows a step by step manner and contains three decision points thus the decision maker can see why a decision path is selected at each step until a final solution is reached. The detailed design of the decision framework is introduced in Chap. 7.

## 1.4 Outline of the Book

Chapter 2 is a literature review about business process modelling, business rule modelling, business rule integration approaches, and business process model understanding. First, we present the fundamental concepts of business process models and factors that affect business process understanding. Then we introduce business rules, which play an important role in process understanding, including the definitions and classifications of business rules. Finally, we introduce the arguments for the integration of business process modes and business rules, and three types of integration approaches.

Chapter 3 introduces the overall research design of this thesis. The research consists of three studies and the methodology of each study is introduced in turn. Study 1 is an experiment empirically evaluating if business rule integration can improve business process model understanding. Study 2 is an exploratory study identifying and evaluating factors that will influence the decision of whether or not a business rule should be integrated with a business process model. Study 3 consists of design science research, developing a decision framework that guides modellers on whether or not to integrate a business rule with a business process model.

Chapter 4 introduces the theoretical underpinning of Study 1. Chapter 4 contributes to business process modelling research by providing a theoretical basis for exploring the effect of integrating business process models and business rules on the understanding of business processes. In this chapter, we introduce a 4-stage cognition process in the context of process and rule modelling, viz. awareness, locating, comprehension and integration, and adopt cognitive theories, including cognitive load theory, information representation theory, and information integration theory, to explore each stage. The theoretical analysis indicates that the integration of business process models with business rules can improve awareness of business rules, reduce cognitive effort and reduce errors in the locating of business rules and the mental integration of business process models and business rules. Further, the representation of business rules in diagrammatic form is more explicit for comprehension than sentential representation.

Chapter 5 introduces the experiment part of Study 1. In this chapter, the study aimed to determine the effect that linked rules have on user understanding of a business process model. We focused on three aspects of understanding: accuracy, time efficiency, and mental effort. Our results suggested that the use of rule links has a positive effect on all three aspects of understanding as compared to process models with associated rules that are separately available. Second, we found that while rule links can reduce time spent per visit overall, which is mainly caused by the reduction of time spent per visit in the Rules Area, it will not increase the overall number of attention switches in the three areas. Instead, rule links can increase visits to the Process Model Area while decreasing visits to the Rules Area.

Chapter 6 introduces the identification and evaluation of factors that can affect the decision to integrate business process modelling and business rule modelling. First we present the methodology for factor identification, evaluation and decision analysis. Then we present the factors, and this is followed by the empirical evaluation of the factors. Finally, we provide six guidelines of rule integration based on the data analysis from the evaluation.

Chapter 7 introduces how we developed the decision framework following the design science research process. We briefly introduce the identification of the problem, which is the lack of guidelines for deciding whether a business rule should be integrated with a business process model; and the definition of the objective, which is to develop a decision framework that can help modellers to make decisions. As a key part of design science is the underlying knowledge that informs the design and development of the artefact, we introduce the knowledge building process as a new step in the design of the decision framework. Then we introduce the decision framework itself with demonstration, and explain how the decision framework can be evaluated.

Chapter 8 concludes the thesis with a discussion of main contributions, limitations and future works. The contributions of this thesis to the body of knowledge of business process and business rule modelling fall into three parts. Study 1 contributes to the body of knowledge by showing that linked rules can improve the understanding of process models in terms of understanding accuracy, understanding time efficiency, and mental effort needed for understanding. Study 2 contributes to the body of knowledge by identifying and evaluating factors that can affect the decision of whether or not to integrate a rule with a business process model. Study 3 contributes to the knowledge by developing a decision framework which can help modellers to make informed decisions as to whether or not a business rule should be integrated with a business process model in practice.

# Chapter 2
# Literature Review

## 2.1 Overview

This chapter first presents the fundamental concepts of business process models and factors that affect business process model understanding. Then we introduce business rules, which play an important role in process understanding, and we include the definitions and classifications of business rules. Finally, we introduce the arguments for the integration of business process models and business rules, and three types of integration approaches.

## 2.2 Business Process Models

A business process is "a collection of activities that takes one or more kinds of input and creates an output that is of value to the customer" [1]. The related activities are structured to accomplish a specific goal that will create value for the organization. A business process model is a graphical representation of a business process, defining the ways in which operations are carried out to accomplish the specific objectives of an organization. Business process modelling is a process of extracting, organizing and representing business activities to guide the analysis, implementation and evolvement of business processes (Harmon and Wolf 2011).

Business process models play a key role in several information systems' management activities. First, a business process model is used to design and understand a business process. While making a process model, the modeller can view the process from various perspectives, and design the process according to requirements. Stakeholders can use a process model to structure, discuss, and share an understanding of business practice among one another. The process models enable users to "play out" different scenarios and thus enable the designer to make modifications and justifications according to the feedback. Process models are also

© Springer Nature Switzerland AG 2019                                        9
W. Wang, *Integrating Business Process Models and Rules*, LNBIP 343,
https://doi.org/10.1007/978-3-030-11809-9_2

used to describe process aware information systems as a "contract" between the system development team and the end users, and are documented as knowledge for training purposes. Second, model based compliance checking can ensure that the designed business practices will be in compliance with regulations and procedures at the stage of model design, rather than detect a non-compliance form of behaviour from process execution logs after it happened. Third, model based performance simulation can be used to understand the factors influencing response time, service level and other performance indicators.

**BPM Life Cycle**

Business process models play an important role in the Business Process Management (BPM) Life Cycle [24]. As illustrated in Fig. 2.1, the BPM Life Cycle consists of five steps, viz. Model, Implement, Execute, Monitor, and Optimize. The Model step captures the business processes at a high level. At this step, just enough detail to understand conceptually how the process works, will be gathered to ensure the high level detail is correct. In the Implement step, the model will be extended to capture more detail required to execute the process, such as the content of messages, and the layout of forms. In the Execute step, instances of the process are launched and executed, automatically, or interacted with by the end users. The Monitor step measures the process performance by using key performance indicators. Statistics are demonstrated graphically on dashboards, and textually in reports to show the bottlenecks and inefficiencies in the process. The Optimize step improves the process by tuning and changing it, then incorporates the changes into the model and repeats the cycle for continuous business process improvement.

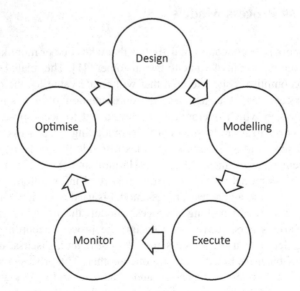

**Fig. 2.1.** Business Process Management life cycle

## Business Process Modelling Languages

Today, there are many conceptual business process modelling languages available. In a process modelling language, processes are modelled graphically, with activities represented as nodes or boxes, which are connected by control flow arcs or arrows [25]. The Business Process Modelling Notation[1] (BPMN[1]) is one example of such a modelling language and it is now a de-facto international process modelling standard [26]. Common constructs in BPMN include events, activities, decision gateways, connectors and swim-lanes, with these then arranged into graphical models through the act of process modelling. For example, Fig. 2.2 shows a pizza ordering and delivering process model represented in BPMN. A pizza customer and a vendor are classified as participants, represented using dedicated, respective pools. The process starts with the pizza customer, who felt hungry and ordered a pizza. After that the customer waited for one of two different events that could happen, as indicated by the event gateway. If the pizza was delivered, the customer would pay and eat the pizza; while if the pizza was not delivered within 60 min, the customer would ask for the pizza every 60 min until the pizza was delivered. The vendor pools have three swim lanes, i.e. the clerk, the chef, and the delivery boy. The clerk receives the order and hands it over to the chef to cook, and calms down the customer if the pizza is not delivered in time. The chef bakes the pizza according to the order and hands it over to the delivery boy. After the pizza is baked, the delivery boy delivers the pizza and receives the payment.

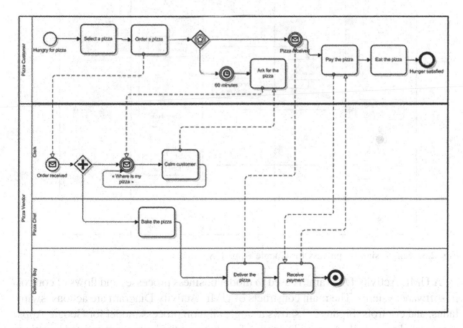

**Fig. 2.2.** BPMN example [27]

---

[1]Business Process Model and Notation (BPMN) is a graphical representation for specify-ing business processes in a business process model.

Besides BPMN, there are other modelling languages, including UML Activity Diagram, Event Driven Process Chain (EPC), and Petri Net.

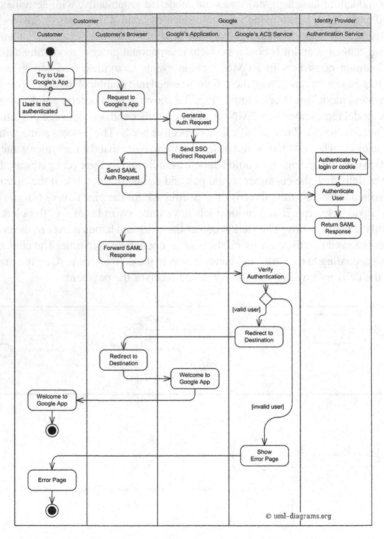

**Fig. 2.3.** Single sign on process for Google Apps [28]

A UML Activity Diagram[2] is used to model business processes and flows of control in software systems. The main constructs of UML Activity Diagram are actions, swim lanes, and controls. Figure 2.3 shows a single sign on process model for Google Apps represented as a UML Activity Diagram. The three participants are presented by using pools, and within each pool, each swim lane represents an actor such as a customer's

---

[2]http://www.uml-diagrams.org/activity-diagrams.html.

browser or Google's ACS Service. When a user attempts to use some hosted Google application, Google generates a SAML authentication request and sends a redirect request back to the user's browser. Then the customer's browser sends a SAML authentication request to the authentication service to authenticate the user. The authentication service returns the SAML response to the browser, and the browser forwards the response to Google's ACS service for verification. If the verification is successful, the customer's browser is redirected to the Google application the customer intends to use, while if the verification fails, an error page will be shown to the customer.

An Event-driven Process Chain (EPC) [29] is a type of flowchart used for business process modelling, which is developed within the ARIS framework. The main constructs of an event-driven process chain are events and functions. Events are passive elements describing the conditions under which a function works. Functions are active elements that modelling tasks and activities. Figure 2.4 is an order shipment process model represented in EPC. In Fig. 2.4, functions are represented in rectangles, while events are represented in hexagons. The process steps behind an OR-Splitter are alternatives, aka at least one of the options has to be selected. The OR-Connector joins the alternative chains again. In the example, after the event "articles are not available" occurred, two reactions could be executed under discretion: production of new articles, or the purchasing of articles from a third party supplier, or performance of both steps. After any one of these options is executed, the order can be shipped.

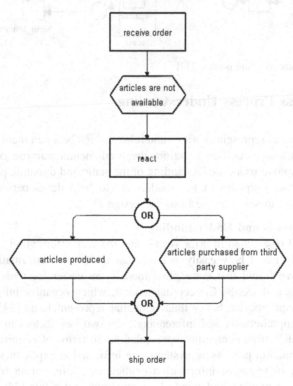

**Fig. 2.4.** Order shipment process [30]

Petri Net [31] is a mathematical modelling language for the description of distributed systems and is utilized for concurrent and nondeterministic process modelling and mathematical process analysis. The main constructs of Petri Net are places, transitions, tokens and arcs. Places represent possible states of the system. Transitions are events or actions which cause the change of state. Arcs run from a place to a transition, or vice versa. Tokens move from one place to another place. Figure 2.5 is a complaint handling process represented in Petri Net. In Fig. 2.5, places are represented as circles and transitions are represented as rectangles. Tokens are presented in hollow circles inside places. In Fig. 2.5, first, an incoming complaint is recorded. Then the client or the department affected is contacted. The data are gathered and assessed. Depending on the assessment result, either a compensation payment is made, or a letter is given to the customer to file the complaint.

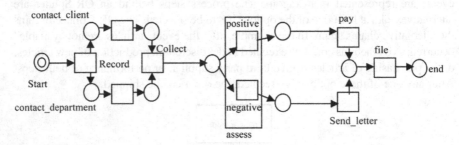

**Fig. 2.5.** Complaint handling process [32]

## 2.3   Business Process Understanding

A conceptual model represents entities and relationships between them in a problem domain. Regardless of chosen notation, the fundamental purpose of conceptual models is to improve users' understanding of the static and dynamic phenomena in a domain. Further purposes of the models are to help developers and users to communicate and to serve as the basis for design [33].

**Conceptual Models and Understanding**
It has been well researched in prior works, that the way information is represented can significantly affect how easily humans can understand information [34, 35]. Researchers have found that conceptual models are easier for understanding, in contrast to texts and words. Conceptual models, which organize information into pictures and diagrams, are better than sentential representations [34] in terms of information comprehension and inferencing. The two key factors that distinguish conceptual models from sentential representations in terms of cognition efficiency in human information processing systems, are information explicitness and search efficiency [35]. In terms of information explicitness, information represented in diagrams is more explicit and needs less computational effort [34]. In contrast,

informationally equivalent representation of the same content but in a sentential form, typically requires further mental formulation to make it explicit for use, which requires greater computational cognitive effort [34, 35]. In terms of search efficiency, in a diagrammatic representation, information is organized by location. Information elements that are relevant are grouped together, and information elements needed for inference are often present at adjacent locations, or connected with associations. Relations between graphical elements map onto the relations of information elements in such a way that they restrict or enforce the kinds of interpretations that can be made [34]. This information-grouping and connecting nature of diagrams makes problem solving proceed through a smooth traversal of the diagram, in which little cognitive effort in terms of search computation is required [35]. In a sentential representation, information is often organized as a list of text items. Finding the relevant information item that matches the conditions of inferences requires searching linearly down the list, and the several items needed may be widely dispersed.

UML and ER are two typical structure modelling languages, focusing on the modelling of software systems and databases respectively [36]. Factors affecting the understanding of UML diagrams and ER diagrams have been widely studied in the past. To name a few, Burton-Jones and Meso [37] studied the effect of the decomposition of UML models on model understanding, and found that better decomposition of UML diagrams following the Good Decomposition Model [38] can increase analysts' understanding of a domain, indicated by higher scores in problem-solving tests and cloze tests. Burton-Jones et al. [39] studied the effect of optional properties in UML class diagrams, following the ontological analysis of optionality in [40] and [41]. They found that the use of optional properties could lead to a loss of semantics about the scopes of properties. Although subclasses with mandatory properties could lead to cognitive difficulties associated with having too much complexity in a model, mandatory properties is a better choice than optional properties. Another piece of research by Burton-Jones and Meso [37] studied the combination effects of model decomposition quality and multiple forms of information on model understanding. Class diagrams, use case diagrams, and state machine diagrams were used in the experiment. They found that multiple forms of information and higher quality decompositions can significantly affect individuals' superficial and deep understanding. Individuals found a domain easier to understand given multiple forms of information, but they did not feel that the domain was easier to understand when given a higher quality decomposition. Allen and March [42] studied the effects of state-based and event-based modelling methods on ER diagrams. The state-based modelling method focuses on things and their descriptions, viewing databases as a snapshot of realty, while the event based method focuses on events and the affected resources and agent, viewing databases as components of transactions [42]. The research asked participants to write SQL quires given state-based and event-based ER diagrams respectively, and found that an event-based E-R diagram can lead users to more accurately recognize when queries they have formulated are correct. Bodart et al. [43] studied the effect of optional properties in ER diagrams. The results they found are in accordance with the study of UML class diagrams in [39] that the use of optional properties should be circumspect in ER diagrams, even though the use of optional properties can enable designers to draw simpler conceptual models. Furthermore, the research points out that if the ER diagrams are to be used to have an overview of the application domain, ER diagrams based on optional properties can provide a satisfactory representation of a domain. If ER diagrams are to be used to support deep-level cognitive processing by their users, optional properties should be proscribed. Shanks et al. [44] studied the effect of two ways (either as relationships or entities) to represent composites in ER diagrams. Their research found that a composite should be represented as an entity class and not modelled implicitly as an association class. Otherwise, users' understanding of the real-world phenomena being represented will be undermined.

**Process Model Understanding Factors**
Process models are a typical type of conceptual model, and the factors affecting the understanding of process models have been well studied. A variety of factors affecting the understanding of process models have been identified and can be classified into two categories: process model factors and individual factors. Process model factors are about the metrics of the process models, such as modularization, block structuredness, and complexity. Individual factors, or personal factors, are about the factors of process model users, such as individual's domain knowledge, modelling knowledge, modelling experience, and education level.

Modularization is found to be a factor affecting the understanding of process models. Modularization is investigated via several forms, including sub-processes, and block structuredness. Reijers et al. [45] and Turetken et al. [46] found that modularized processes, in particular, process models with sub-processes, are easier to understand compared to flattened process models. La Rosa et al. [47] found that block structuredness can affect process model understanding. A block structure is a part of a process model enclosed by a splitting element and a joining element. Despite the degree of modularization, the quality of modularization has been studied as well. The quality of modularization is concerned with whether a process model is modularized according to certain guidelines. Johannsen et al. [48] and Zugal et al. [49] found that models that comply with decomposition guidelines such as minimality, determinism and losslessness are easier to understand compared to models that violate these guidelines, which is consistent with the research in [33] on general conceptual models. Minimality means that modules do not contain redundant or unnecessary elements. Determinism means modules are interacting in a well-defined manner. Losslessness means modules are representing all relevant emergent properties.

Complexity is another important factor that has been studied by many. Different works have focused on different forms of complexity, and all these complexities contribute to the decreased understandability of process models. The independent variables investigated in the work on complexity include: number of arcs and nodes [50, 51], number of gateways [45, 52, 53], number of events [52], number of loops [54], and number of concurrencies [55], length of the longest path [53, 55], depth of nesting [56], and gateway heterogeneity [53, 55]. Number of concurrencies means the number of paths that should be executed in parallel. Length of the longest path means the longest of the paths connecting the beginning and the end of a process model. Depth of nesting means the maximum level at which a sub-process or process block enclosed by splitting and joining elements is nested in the outer process. Gateway heterogeneity means the number of different types of gateways that are used in a model.

Other factors affecting process model understanding include symbol color systems [57], syntax highlighting [45], label styles [58], label abstractness [54], and label length [55]. Symbol color systems use different colors for different symbols. Syntax highlighting highlights matching operator pairs, such as split-join pairs in different colors. Research has found that process models with symbol color systems have lower perceived understanding difficulty, and syntax-highlighting can improve process understanding accuracy compared with single color and non-syntax-highlighting process models. Labels are classified into verb-objective style (like *Process an Order*), action-noun style (like *Order Processing*) and other styles (like *Status Analysis Cash Position*) in [58]. The research in [58] showed that verb-object label style was rated highest in perceived usefulness, followed by action-noun label style, and finally the rest of the labels. Research in [54] showed that abstract label was related to higher understanding accuracy and lower time taken for understanding. Mendling and Strembeck [55] found that the length of text in labels is negatively related to understanding accuracy – i.e. the longer the texts were, the lower the understanding accuracy achieved.

A number of individual factors affect the understanding of process models, including domain knowledge, modelling knowledge, experience, education level, training level, verbal and visual cognitive style, and learning style. The effect of domain knowledge and modelling knowledge has been studied extensively [46, 54, 59–62]. Domain knowledge includes the knowledge of the domain and practice. Modelling knowledge includes knowledge of modelling languages and modelling methods. Although positively correlated, the results have shown that domain knowledge and modelling knowledge had no significant effect on comprehension accuracy. Similarly, the correlation between experience and process model understanding is not significant [50, 61]. Experience is measured by the number of years the participant has been involved in process modelling [50].

On the other hand, education level [63], training level [60], individuals' cognitive style [64], and learning style [62] have been proven to play important roles in model understanding. In a process model understanding experiment, Reijers et al. [65] found that graduate students achieved significantly better understanding than undergraduate students. Figl et al. [60] found that training in process modelling basics among university students can significantly influence their understanding accuracy and cognitive load. The cognitive style of learning was classified into verbal style, spatial style, and objective style in [64]. Each learning style accounts for the processing of information in different ways. The verbal style of learning involves processing of information in words; the spatial style in object locations and spatial relationships, and the object style, in information about the visual appearance of objects, including their shape, color, and texture. The research results in [64] showed that users of the spatial style of learning preferred diagrams over text, while the experiment participants with verbal styles preferred text over diagrams, and preferred structured text over text. Participants with object style of learning had no significant preference. The intuitive learning style individuals prefer to learn relations and concepts in a holistic way, while those favouring a sensing learning style prefer to learn and memorize facts bit-by-bit [62]. The research in [62] showed that participants with a sensing learning style achieved better process model understanding in terms of comprehension accuracy than participants with an intuitive learning style.

## 2.4  Business Rules

Along with business process models, business rules are another type of model that focusses on the capturing of organizational practice.

**Business Rule Definitions**
There are several different views of what a business rule is. Ceri [66] stated that business rules model the reactions to events which occur in practice, with tangible side effects on the database content, so as to encapsulate the application's reactive behaviour in relation to such events. Hay et al. [67] defined a business rule as a statement that defines or constrains some aspect of the business. It is intended to assert business structure or to control or influence the behaviour of the business. Selfridge [68] defined a business rule as a requirement on the conditions or manipulation of data expressed in terms of the business enterprise or application domain. Rosca [69] defined the requirements that determine or affect how a business is run as business rules. In other words, business rules are statements about the enterprise's way of doing business. They reflect policies, procedures or other constraints on ways to satisfy customers, make good use of resources, and conform to laws or business conventions and the like [69].

**Business Rule Classifications**
Business rules can be classified into different categories from different aspects. Nayak et al. [4] classified business rules into structural business behavioural business rules. Structural business rules describe relationships and constraints among data elements. For example, "a customer can have at most 3 credit cards" is a structural business rule. Behavioural business rules describe the governing principles of process execution, such as execution pathways and user privileges. For example, "a transaction should be verified by a manager if the amount is over 10,000" is a behavioural business rule. Do Prado Leite and Leonardi [70] classified business rules as functional rules and non-functional rules. Functional rules are the rules regarding organization actions. For example, "the supervisors have to report to

the director" is a function rule. Non-functional rules are relationships or standards that must be observed by the organization. For example, "the salary of a senior employee must be greater than the salary of a junior employee" is a non-functional rule. Giblin et al. [71] classified business rules as enforceable rules and non-enforceable rules. Enforceable rules can also be monitored and enforced in systems. Enforceable rules can be enforced in systems. Non-enforceable rules are further classified into monitorable and non-monitorable rules. Violations of monitorable but non-enforceable rules cannot be prevented, they can at least be detected. For example, "the defect rate of product A should be lower than 1‰" is a non-enforceable rule, but can be monitored in the production process. Additional measures are needed for non-enforceable and non-monitorable rules to achieve compliance, which are typically external to the system. For example, "a customer need to tell whether the manufacture process of a product has already commenced when the order is cancelled" is a non-enforceable and non-monitorable rule because a customer normally does not have access to such kind of internal information [72]. Zur Muehlen and Indulska [5] classified business rules from the source aspect into mandates, policies, and guidelines. Mandates are rules from laws and must be followed and ensured. For example, "payable taxes must be payed in time" is a mandate. Policies are company rules that should be followed. For example, "the budget of the new project cannot exceed 10,000" is a policy. Guidelines are rules that may or may not apply depending on circumstances. For example, "candidate system managers should have a master degree in computer science" is a guideline in a hiring position, as this requirement can be left alone given that a candidate has a rich experience as a system manager. Wagner [73] classified business rules from the structural aspect into integrity rules, derivation rules, reaction rules, production rules, and transformation rules. An integrity rule is a constraint specifying the quantitative relationship between two entities. For example, "a project must have one and only one project manager" is an integrity rule. A derivation rule is a statement containing a condition and a conclusion. For example "a platinum customer is a customer who has a credit equal to or over 5,000 points" is a derivation rule. "A credit equal to or over 5,000 points" is the condition, and "platinum customer" is the conclusion. A reaction rule is a statement consists of an event, a condition, and an action. For example, "when an invoice is received, if the invoice amount is more than 1,000 dollars, the invoice should be forwarded to a supervisor" is a reaction rule. "An invoice is received" is an event, "the invoice amount is more than 1,000 dollars" is a condition, and "forwarded to a supervisor" is the corresponding action. A production rule consists of a condition and a conclusion. For example, "if there are no defects in the last batch of cars, then the batch is approved" is a production rule. "No defects in the last batch of cars" is a condition, and "the batch is approved" is the corresponding conclusion. A transformation rule is a statement about the lawful change of states. For example, "an employee's age can increase, but cannot decrease" is a transformation rule. Increase is the lawful change of an employee's age.

**Business Rule Modelling Languages**

There are several options for modelling business rules. SBVR (Semantics of Business Vocabulary and Business Rules) is a rule modelling language adopted by Object Management Group as a standard. SBVR is intended to formalize complex compliance rules that can be interpreted and used by computer systems. It provides an unambiguous, meaning-centric, multilingual, and semantically rich capability for defining meanings of the language used by people in an industry, profession, discipline, field of study, or organization. SBVR documents are expressed in structured natural language. SBVR specifications can be transformed into IT specifications, such as database schemas, rules and workflow models and operation manuals.

SBVR rules are based on fact types, and fact types are based on terms. A fact type is turned into a rule by adding a modal operator, and then quantifiers and qualifiers. For example, in a business rule specified in SBVR that "it is permitted that a rental is open only if an estimated rental charge is provisionally charged to a credit card of the renter that is responsible for the rental", "rental", "rental charge", and "credit card" are terms; "rental has rental charge" is a fact type; "only if" is the qualifier; "a" is the quantifier; and "it is permitted" is the modal operator.

The REWERSE Rule Markup Language (R2ML) is developed by the REWERSE Working Group to interchange rules between systems and tools. R2ML supports integrity rules, derivation rules, production rules and reaction rules. R2ML allows structure-preserving markup and does not force users to translate their rule expressions into different language paradigms. R2ML can be deployed to different platform-specific rule languages such as RuleML, Drools, and OCL by means of translators. Figure 2.6 is the representation of the following integrity rule in R2ML: "A preferred client must have a portfolio that includes at least three products (for example, a preferred client may have a portfolio that includes vehicle and life insurance policies and an individual retirement account)". As seen in Fig. 2.6, Line 1 is the r2ml:RuleBase element which declares the parent of this rule set (Line 2). This integrity rule is represented in a DeonticIntegrityRule element (Line 4). A Documentation (Lines 5–8) contains the rule text. The rule is an implication that embeds a Logical Formula without free variables. Lines 13–35 introduce the conditions (the antecedent element) of the rule. All the atoms that form the rule are connected by r2ml:Conjunction. The rule conditions are expressed using ReferencePropertyAtom (Lines 15–22 and 25–32). The conditions are enclosed in an AtLeastQuantifiedFormula element (Line 23) with the attribute r2ml: minCardinality="3", representing the "at least three products" in the rule. A ReferencePropertyAtom associates a subject and an object. A consequent element (Lines 36–43) follows the antecedent element. The conclusion is a classification of the client object variable to an userv:PreferredClient class.

```
<r2ml:RuleBase
xmlns:r2ml="http://www.rewerse.net/I1/2006/R2ML"
xmlns:dc="http://purl.org/dc/elements/1.1/"

xmlns:userv="http://www.businessrulesforum.com/2005/userv
#"
  xmlns:xsi="http://www.w3.org/2001/XMLSchema-instance"
  xsi:schemaLocation="http://www.rewerse.net/I1/2006/R2ML
http://oxygen.informatik.tu-cottbus.de/R2ML/0.5/R2ML.xsd"
<r2ml:IntegrityRuleSet
r2ml:ruleSetID="UServIntegrityRuleSet"
  r2ml:externalVocabulary="http://oxygen.informatik.tu-
cottbus.de/rewerse-i1/files/UServ_IAR.jpg"
  r2ml:externalVocabularyLanguage="UML">
<r2ml:DeonticIntegrityRule r2ml:ruleID="CC_01">
 <r2ml:Documentation>
  <r2ml:RuleText r2ml:textFormat="plain">
  <![CDATA[A preferred client must have a portfolio that
in-cludes at least three products (for example, a pre-
ferred client may have a portfolio that includes vehicle
and life insurance policies and an individual retirement
account).]]>
  </r2ml:RuleText>
 </r2ml:Documentation>
 <r2ml:constraint>
  <r2ml:UniversallyQuantifiedFormula>
   <r2ml:ObjectVariable r2ml:name="client"
r2ml:class="userv:Client"/>
   <r2ml:Implication>
    <r2ml:antecedent>
     <r2ml:Conjunction>
      <r2ml:ReferencePropertyAtom
r2ml:referenceProperty="userv:hasPortfolio">
       <r2ml:subject>
        <r2ml:ObjectVariable r2ml:name="client"
r2ml:class="userv:Client"/>
       </r2ml:subject>
       <r2ml:object>
        <r2ml:ObjectVariable r2ml:name="portfolio"
r2ml:class="userv:Portfolio"/>
       </r2ml:object>
      </r2ml:ReferencePropertyAtom>
      <r2ml:AtLeastQuantifiedFormula
r2ml:minCardinality="3">
       <r2ml:ObjectVariable r2ml:name="product"
r2ml:class="userv:Product"/>
       <r2ml:ReferencePropertyAtom
r2ml:referenceProperty="userv:hasProduct">
        <r2ml:subject>
         <r2ml:ObjectVariable r2ml:name="portfolio"
```

**Fig. 2.6.** R2ML illustration [74]

```
r2ml:class="userv:Portfolio"/>
        </r2ml:subject>
        <r2ml:object>
         <r2ml:ObjectVariable r2ml:name="product"/>
        </r2ml:object>
       </r2ml:ReferencePropertyAtom>
      </r2ml:AtLeastQuantifiedFormula>
     </r2ml:Conjunction>
    </r2ml:antecedent>
    <r2ml:consequent>
     <r2ml:ObjectClassificationAtom
r2ml:class="userv:PreferredClient">
       <r2ml:ObjectVariable r2ml:name="client"/>
      </r2ml:ObjectClassificationAtom>
     </r2ml:consequent>
    </r2ml:Implication>
   </r2ml:UniversallyQuantifiedFormula>
  </r2ml:constraint>
  </r2ml:DeonticIntegrityRule>
 </r2ml:IntegrityRuleSet>
</r2ml:RuleBase>
```

**Fig. 2.6.** (continued)

## 2.5   Business Process Model and Business Rule Integration

Business process models and business rule models both focus on the capturing of organizational practice. They are complementary approaches as they address distinct aspects of organizational practices. Zur Muehlen et al. [5] conducted a representation capacity analysis of business process and business rule modelling languages including BPMN, EPC, Petri-Net, SBVR and SRML using the BWW framework [75], finding that none of the languages analysed can provide a complete coverage for all BWW constructs. The overlap analysis shows that the representation capacity of process modelling languages such as BPMN can be enriched by the addition of SRML or SBVR, which is in line with early speculations in [13] and the research finding in [6] that in practice, there is a deficiency in BPMN for modelling business rules.

While process models can incorporate more complex business rules, in practice, due to limited support for representation of business rules in graphical process modelling techniques [6], organizations represent these rules in natural language (or one of the main business rule modelling languages – e.g. [7, 8]) and often store such representations in separate text documents, spreadsheets, or disconnected business rule repositories. Such separation of process models and rules creates a high risk for decision making, in that any decisions made on the basis of the graphical models alone are made on the basis of incomplete information. In such a situation, where there is a separation of graphical process models and business rules, it is easy to be unaware of corresponding rules when investigating a process model, and also hard to locate the correct corresponding rules in a separate source. Since the pieces of information from a process model and corresponding rules are not physically integrated, even if the users are aware of the separate sources of information, they need to integrate the information mentally, which imposes additional cognitive effort on searching and locating rules, interpreting the relevance between each specific rule and a specific activity, and structuring a holistic mental representation of the information. This situation gives rise to a risk of users inadvertently breaching required standards of operation or making ill-informed decisions because they lack awareness of all rules governing a given process. Different stakeholders, such as process designers, information systems developers, and process participants may have inconsistent or even conflicting understandings of the same process. Ultimately, this situation hinders the effectiveness of many important organizational activities, such as developing a shared understanding, effective communication, knowledge management, process improvement, and decision-making, and also introduces risks of noncompliant process execution.

We noted that Krogstie et al. [76] were the first to motivate and discuss integrated modelling of business processes and business rules. Many arguments for the integration of business process models and business rules occurred after them. We summarize the arguments into four categories, viz. model completeness, understandability and communication, improved governance, risk and compliance, and process flexibility. In the following, we provide an overview of each argument indicated in the literature.

Model Completeness. Business process modelling and business rule modelling are two common aspects of the conceptual modelling of information systems [77]. "Integration between business processes and business rules is necessary for applications which not only hold numerous business knowledge or policies but also need the intercommunication among some distributed and heterogeneous components" [78]. A basic requirement of a model is its completeness in representing the real world. A complete process model represents all key aspects of a business process and thus is a high quality business process model [79], which cannot be achieved without integrating all business rules with business process models.

Understanding and Communication. Business rules constitute an entire body of knowledge and have not been adequately addressed in business process modelling notations [80]. Typically, business rules are buried in the program code or in database structures [80]. The gap between business process modelling and specification of business rules may lead to misunderstandings while reading and interpreting business models, and communication issues [81]. Some of these issues can be resolved by the integration of business process models and business rules [9]. The separation of processes and rules makes communication between organizations difficult because the process models used for communication do not represent all information about relevant business activities. Integrated and complete information should be provided in the business process model for inter-organizational communication and collaboration. Integration of business process models and business rules is further identified as a need for the intercommunication between distributed and heterogeneous components [78].

Improved Governance, Risk and Compliance. Compliance means that business processes are in accordance with a prescribed set of norms [82]. Compliance requirements are interpreted and transformed into rules to ensure that the operation of the organization aligns with requirements. Organisations struggle to establish a consistent view of their policies and operating procedures in the heavily constrained business world [11]. The separation of process models and business rules further complicates the development of a consistent view of policies and operating procedures and thus increases the risk of non-compliant activities and the difficulty of showing compliant process design [11]. Processes need to comply with business rules to ensure that the processes are error-free at the modelling level [12]. Without integration of business rules and process models, it is possible for the user to act based on the activities in the model only, not realizing that additional constraints exist.

Process Flexibility. The dynamic environment of organizations makes business processes subject to frequent change [83]. In practice, business process models and business rules are either kept in separated repositories, which make review and assessment a difficult task, or mixed together, which decreases the configurability and flexibility of processes [84]. Prior research has indicated that integration of business process models and business rules can improve the flexibility of business processes [85]. The lack of comprehensive representation for business rules makes business process modelling notations problematic for modelling complex business logics and makes it hard to meet frequently changing business requirements. Thus the flexibility, adaptability and dynamism of business processes, which are emerging requirements for enterprise information systems, are difficult to achieve [83].

## 2.6 Integration Approaches

Over the past two decades, the need to model business rules in an integrated manner with business processes has been argued theoretically [5, 15] as well as validated empirically [16, 17]. A variety of integration methods [11, 15, 18–23] have been developed since researchers first suggested that business process and rule modelling approaches should be merged [76]. To name a few, [77] defined the structure of rules to couple business process models and rules. Knolmayer et al. [3] refined process modelling and linked the resulting models to workflow execution through layers of Reaction Business Rules. Kovacic and Groznik [2] developed a meta-model to demonstrate how rules can link process, activity, events, data objects, and software components. Milanovic et al. [21] introduced an integrated modelling language rBPMN, which is a combination of BPMN and R2ML to model flexible business process models. Habich et al. [15] proposed an integrated approach to join rules and processes from a modelling and execution perspective. Their solution includes the enhancement of business processes with SBVR annotations, automatic integration of SBVR vocabulary with business process models, and transformation of business rules to OCL constraints.

We conducted an analysis of related literature to determine the main approaches for integrated business process and rule modelling. Our analysis has identified three main approaches. To summarize, three forms of integration of business process models and rules have been developed in the literature *viz*. link, text embedding, and diagrammatic embedding. These approaches are explained in the following.

**Link.** Link means information about the location of a related rule is provided in a process model. A link can be clicked to automatically navigate to the corresponding rule. The link integration method can use several modelling constructs to convey the link information. Sapkota and van Sinderen [18], and Kluza et al. [19] used BPMN activity, and gateway constructs respectively, to implement the link information, as shown in Fig. 2.7(a)–(c) respectively. In [18], rules are externalized and linked to the decision point activity of a process model. Flexibility can be achieved by attaching or removing rules from a process model.

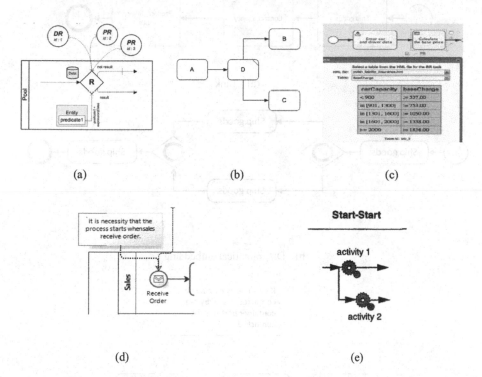

**Fig. 2.7.** Integration methods illustration

**Text Embedding.** Text integration is the representation of a business rule in textual form in a graphical business process model. For example, BPMN has a text annotation construct which allows users to specify business rules in such an annotation construct, in sentential format. For example, in [11], an annotation based mapping method is introduced to find out which BPMN constructs are used for

SBVR rules and where the access points are in a BPMN diagram so as to insert relative rules as annotations, thus providing a consolidated and consistent view of organizational policies and operating procedures, as shown in Fig. 2.7(d).

**Diagrammatic Embedding.** Diagrammatic integration represents the business rules logic in a graphical format, using process modelling constructs such as sequence flows and gateways. For example, [23] developed several constructs to express the activity ordering policies which do not exist in current graphical process modelling languages. These policies are a combination of dependencies such as start-start and end-start, and control structures such as sequence, branching and joining. Figure 2.7(e) shows the start-start pattern of a sequence control structure.

Figure 2.8 illustrates the three different rule integration approaches on the same process models.

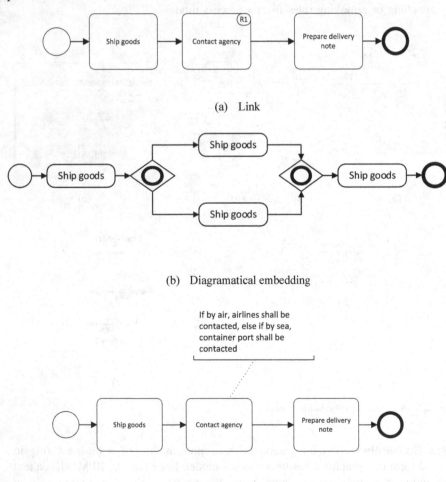

(a)  Link

(b)  Diagramatical embedding

(c)  Text embedding

**Fig. 2.8.** Integration approaches illustration

While both linking and embedding can be used as integration approaches, there are some important differences between the two. Link approaches are more flexible than process-based embedding approaches [18]. In link approaches, flexibility is achieved because the rules are executed directly by the rule engine and hence they can be added or removed when needed; whereas in process-based approaches, any addition or removal of activities requires changes in the existing process and hence the underlying implementation [18, 21]. The differences between linking and embedding (including text embedding and diagrammatic embedding) are summarized in Table 2.1.

**Table 2.1.** Rule link and embedding comparison

| Link | Embedding |
|---|---|
| Rules and process models are separately modelled. Rules are not part of a process model, but only connected with a process model | Rules are modelled INSIDE a process model. Rules are regarded as a part of a process model |
| Rules and a process model are managed by different systems, i.e. they are managed by BPMS and BPRS separately | Rules are managed together with a process model by the same system/tool, i.e. a BPMN editor which can edit process models as well as the rules in annotation symbols |
| A linked rule can be accessed separately without the need to access a process model | Access to an embedded rule needs access to the process model |
| A linked rule can be reused without separating it from the process model | An embedded rule first needs to be separated from the process model, then be reused |
| Change to a linked business rule requires less analysis and time than for an embedded rule' Change to one rule will automatically update the same rule embedded in other process models | Change to one rule will not automatically update the same rule embedded in other process models |

Text embedding and diagrammatical embedding are two methods of embedding, and they different from each other in a two ways. On one hand, information representation theory has shown that diagrams are better than sentential representations [34] in terms of information comprehension and inferencing. Information represented in diagrams is more explicit and needs less computational mental effort [34]. In contrast, informationally equivalent representation of the same content but in a sentential form typically requires further mental formulation to make it explicit for use, which requires greater computational cognitive effort [34, 35]. As diagrammatical embedding uses diagrammatical symbols to represent information, it requires less mental effort than text embedding. On the other hand, it is well studied in current literature that not all business rules can be diagrammatically represented in business process models due to the limited representational capacities of current business process modelling languages [5, 6, 8], whereas text embedding has a broader representational capacity.

## 2.7   Chapter Summary

In this chapter, we first introduced the basic concepts of business process models, and the factors that affect business process understanding. Then we introduced the concept of business rules as an important factor that can affect business process understanding, and this was followed by the arguments about the benefits of the integration of business process models and business rules. Finally, three types of integration approaches were introduced.

# Chapter 3
# Methodology

As introduced in Chap. 1, the three objectives of the thesis are to: (1) investigate whether business rule integration can improve business process model under-standing; (2) identify and evaluate factors that will influence the decision of whether or not a business rule should be integrated with a business process model; (3) de-velop a decision framework that guides modellers on whether or not to integrate a business rule with a business process model based on the research results from the first two objectives. Accordingly, we carried out three studies to fulfil each of these objectives:

**Study 1:** An experiment empirically evaluating whether business rule integra-tion can improve business process model understanding.

**Study 2:** An exploratory study identifying and evaluating factors that influence the decision as to whether or not a business rule should be integrated with a business process model.

**Study 3:** A design science based development of a decision framework that guides modellers on whether or not to integrate a business rule with a business process model.

In this chapter, we focus on the explanation of how these three studies are connected to form a thesis, and how and why the research methods of each study were chosen. As the three studies use different research methods, the detailed methods of each study are introduced in Chaps. 5, 6, and 7 separately.

The three studies are interrelated. Study 1 answers the fundamental questions including whether business rule integration can improve business process model understanding, what the motivation of this research is and what the most important benefits of business rule integration are. If business rule integration cannot improve business process model understanding, then there would be no motivation to continue this research. As the decision of whether to integrate business rules with business process models is not a straight forward one, Study 2 aims to identify and evaluate all factors that will influence the decision-making of integrating a business rule with a business process model, apart from understanding. These factors influence whether or not a business rule should be integrated, which integration

© Springer Nature Switzerland AG 2019
W. Wang, *Integrating Business Process Models and Rules*, LNBIP 343,
https://doi.org/10.1007/978-3-030-11809-9_3

approach should be adopted, and what the costs and benefits are. Study 3 designs a decision framework that guides modellers on whether to, and how to integrate a business rule with a business process model, based on the research results from the prior two studies. The first two studies result in the development of a knowledge base for the components design of the third study. The relationships between the three studies are illustrated in Fig. 3.1.

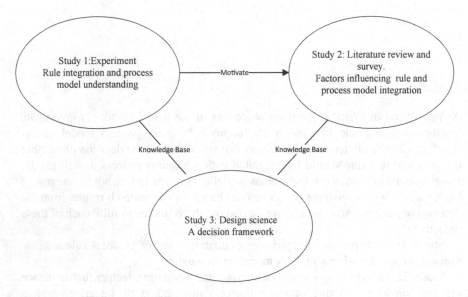

**Fig. 3.1.** The relationship between the three studies

## 3.1   Research Method of Study 1 – Experiment

The objective of Study 1 is to empirically evaluate if business rule integration can improve business process model understanding. This research question is about the causal relationship between two concepts: the representation of business rules and process models (integration of rules with a process model), and the understandability of process models. The most appropriate research method is experiment because experiments are often used to test the causal relationship between the independent variable(s) and the dependent variable(s). In an experiment, there are three kinds of variables, i.e. independent variables, dependent variables, and control variables. An independent variable is a variable that will be studied and changed in an experiment. A dependent variable is a variable that changes correspond to the change of an independent variable. A control is a variable that could influence experiment result but not the focus of a study. Control variables should be kept unchanged throughout an experiment, as any change of a control variable will invalidate the correlation of dependent variables to the independent variable. The control variable strongly influences experimental results, and it is held constant during the experiment in order to test the relative relationship of the dependent and independent variables. Experiments can test if the independent variable(s) and the dependent variable(s) are correlated by manipulating the independent variable(s), while keeping the control variables the same. Other research methods are not suitable for Study 1. Case studies focus on studying a subject in real life settings through a period of time, and includes the complex interaction between the researcher and the many parts of the research environment. Compared with experimentation, in which the independent and dependent variables are determined first, case studies are more explorative, and do not test the correlation between two variables, but rather explore the subject in depth. Thus, case study is not suitable for this study. A Literature review can have substantive findings as well as theoretical and methodological contributions based on current body of knowledge. However, literature reviews are secondary sources, and do not report new or original knowledge. As the question of whether business rule integration can improve business process model understanding has not been empirically evaluated in current body of knowledge, a literature review is not suitable for the study. Survey studies the sampling of individual units from a population by collecting information or opinions from individuals using questionnaires. A survey is often used to collect data that are known and familiar by an individual, such as "how many years of experience you have in process modelling". A survey is not suitable for questions of which the answers are unsure for an individual. For example it is not suitable to ask an individual "can the colour of process model affect process model understanding", as the answer of this question is unknown to an individual if he or she hasn't read any paper about an experiment testing this question. Using a survey to collect data about complex questions which are unknown to participants can result in unreliable data. A focus group is a small group of people whose reactions are studied in guided or open discussions about a new product or something else to determine the reactions that can be expected from a larger population. As a focus group aims to collect data about people's perceptions, opinions, beliefs, and attitudes towards a thing or phenomenon, it is not suitable to collect object data, thus not suitable for this study.

## 3.2 Research Method of Study 2 – Systematic Literature Review and Survey

The objective of Study 2 is to identify and evaluate factors that will influence the decision of whether or not a business rule should be integrated with a business process model. Thus, there are two sub-objectives in Study 2. The first is to identify the factors that can influence the decision of whether a business rule should be integrated with a business process model; and the second is to evaluate the factors.

For the first sub-objective, one of the most important criteria is broad coverage of all possible factors so as to make sure we don't miss out any important factors. If any factor is missing from the identifying stage, it loses the possibility of being included in the decision framework, weakening the validity and usefulness of the decision framework. To rigorously find all possible factors, we adopt the systematic literature review as the research method. A systematic review can provide a complete, exhaustive summary of current literature relevant to our research question. We used a keyword search in our literature database of over 43,000 full-text papers, including core information systems and computer science conference and journal papers to avoid missing any important factor. Other research methods such as interviews or surveys can only be conducted with very limited number of participants, and only knowledge from the selected participants is collected, leading to incomplete results. Large scale interviews or surveys would limit this drawback; however the resources and time needed are not affordable for such a research study in a PhD program.

After the factors are identified, the second sub-objective is to evaluate whether the identified factors are valid and important. To answer this research question, we adopt the survey research method. Particularly we design a questionnaire asking experts to evaluate the factors and use their experience and knowledge to make integration choices. While a survey in the form of interviews or open questions can also be an alternative research method to collect rich data, it is difficult to quantitatively aggregate and analyse the data, as interviews will have qualitative data and heterogonous data structure for each participant. For example it is difficult to rank the factors according to their importance from the data collected by interviewing. As case studies also collect qualitative data, neither are they suitable for this sub-objective. As we identify 12 factors in the factor identification study, evaluating and comparing these factors together in an experiment is not feasible, as experimentation can only handle a few independent variables. Also, not all factors are operationalizable, thus cannot be measured.

## 3.3   Research Method of Study 3 – Design Science

The objective of Study 3 is to develop a decision framework that guides modellers on whether or not to integrate a business rule with a business process model towards achieving the benefits of integrated modelling based on the research results from the first two objectives. As the objective is to design an artefact, the research methodology of Study 3 is Design Science. Design Science is the research method used to create artefacts intended to solve identified problems in practice [86]. The artefacts of design science can be constructs, models, methods and instantiations [87]. In this study, the artefact is the decision framework that will help business rule modellers decide whether to model a business rule with a business process model or not. This study is governed by the guidelines set out within the overarching Design Science paradigm as well as the heuristic problem-solving strategies [87].

We followed a commonly accepted design science research methodology for the production and presentation of design science research in IS [86]. The design science research process includes six activities, viz. problem identification and motivation, objectives definition, design and development, demonstration, evaluation, and communication. Problem identification and motivation is intended to define the specific research problem and justify the value of a solution. Objectives definition is needed to infer the objectives of a solution from the problem definition and knowledge of what is possible and feasible. Design and development relates to creating the artifact, including determining the artifact's desired functionality and its architecture and then creating the actual artifact. Resources required for moving from objectives to design and development include knowledge that can be brought to bear in a solution. Demonstration is needed in order to demonstrate the use of the artifact to solve one or more instances of the problem using experimentation, simulation, case study, proof, or other appropriate methods. Evaluation relates to observations and other investigative means to evaluate how well the artifact supports a solution to the problem. Finally, communication is intended to communicate the problem and the artifact to researchers and other relevant audiences such as practicing professionals when appropriate. The detailed research methodology of Study 3 is introduced in Chap. 7.

## 3.4   Chapter Summary

In this chapter, we presented the overall design of the research. The research consists of three studies. Study 1 is an experiment empirically evaluating if business rule integration can improve business process model understanding. Study 2 is an exploratory study identifying and evaluating factors that influence the decision of whether or not a business rule should be integrated with a business process model. Study 3 is a design science study developing a decision framework that guides modellers on whether or not to integrate a business rule with a business process model.

# Chapter 4
# Rule Integration and Model Understanding: A Theoretical Underpinning

## 4.1 Overview

In Chap. 2 we introduced the arguments for integration and a variety of integration methods. However, whether such integration improves user understanding of the process models has not been investigated. In particular, while researchers have argued that integrated modelling can improve the understanding of business processes, this proposition has neither been theoretically analysed, nor empirically evaluated. Yet, such understanding is crucial for the advancement of process modelling methods. As a lacking of a cognitive model in terms of how model users learn process models and rules in current body of knowledge, in this chapter, we propose a four-stage cognitive process based on a cognitive model in human information searching and processing [88], and explore theoretical foundations that underpin the understanding of process models.

## 4.2 Related Theories

As stated in [89], there are different views of theories in information systems. Theories can be statements that say how something should be done in practice, that provide a lens for viewing or explaining the world, or that declaring relationships among constructs. Here we consider theory as statements that declare the relationships between constructs. We use cognitive load theory and cognitive fit theory to provide a fundamental theory support for our analysis.

Cognitive load theory is built on the widely accepted model of human information processing [90]. It explains the relationships between cognitive load and understanding performance, indicating that the representation of information should minimize cognitive load in problem solving tasks. Cognitive load theory explains the relationship between external problem representation, problem-solving task, mental representation for task solution, and problem-solving performance, indicating that the format of information presentation should match the characteristics of the problem-solving task.

W. Wang, *Integrating Business Process Models and Rules*, LNBIP 343,
https://doi.org/10.1007/978-3-030-11809-9_4

Then we introduce two effects that has been empirically evaluated in literature, which are derived from the two theories and are close related with our analysis of process model understanding. One is that diagrams are easier to understand than text, the other one is the split attention effect. Finally, we use the introduced theories and the evaluated effects to analysis whether the integration of business process models with business rules might improve human understanding of business processes.

**Cognitive Load Theory**

Cognitive load theory is built on the widely accepted information processing model [90] which was proposed by Atkinson et al. The information processing model is shown in Fig. 4.1. Many researchers have added to the understanding of this information processing model, but the basic model remains the same. The information processing model has three main parts, i.e. sensory memory, working memory and long-term memory. Sensory Information are things that the brain collects from our senses (sight, hearing, touch, etc.) that give us information about the world around us. Sensory memory filters out most of this information, and passes the most important items into working memory, where it is either processed or discarded. Working memory can generally hold between five and nine items of information at any one time. When our brain processes information, it categorizes that information and moves it into long-term memory, where it is stored in knowledge structures called schemas. A schema describes a pattern of thought or behaviour that organizes categories of information and the relationships among them. For example, we have schemas for different concepts such as dog, mammal, and animal. Schemas permit us to treat multiple elements as a single element in the working memory. Learning requires a change in the schematic structures of long term memory and the difference between an expert and a novice is that a novice hasn't acquired the schemas of an expert.

Cognitive Load Theory was developed by Sweller [91]. Cognitive load is the construct representing the mental effort that, when a learner performs a particular task, imposes itself on the learner's cognitive system [92, 93]. It includes the amount of information that needs to be held in working memory, and the amount of activities that are required to perform a particular task, including processing and rehearsal information

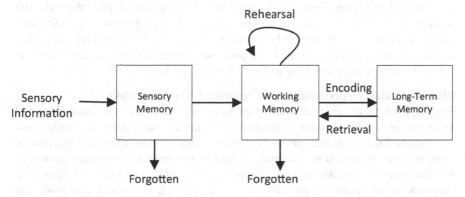

**Fig. 4.1.** Information processing model

in working memory, encoding information, and retrieving information from long-term memory. A Heavy cognitive load can have negative effects on comprehension task completion. It typically creates errors in the process of information comprehension. Cognitive load theory suggests that learning happens best under conditions that are aligned with human cognitive architecture. For the effective understanding of information and for the acquisition of schemas, information should be designed in a way that keep cognitive load of learners at a minimum during the learning process.

Three types of cognitive load can be distinguished. Intrinsic cognitive load is determined by an interaction between the nature of the material being learned and the expertise of the learners. Extraneous cognitive load is the extra load beyond the intrinsic cognitive load, resulting from mainly poorly designed external representations. Germane cognitive load is the load related to processes that contribute to the construction and automation of schemas. While the representation of information cannot affect intrinsic cognitive load, it can be designed to manipulate extraneous and germane load.

**Cognitive Fit Theory**

Cognitive fit theory provides an explanation for performance differences among users across different presentation formats of information, and is widely used as theoretical support in conceptual model understanding studies, such as in [33, 94, 95]. Cognitive fit theory was developed by Vessey [96]. The theory proposes that matching the representation of information with the representation of tasks can improve the performance of tasks for individual users.

Figure 4.2 presents the general problem solving model that the cognitive fit theory is based on. The problem-solving model views problem solving as an outcome of the mental representation for task solution, which is formulated from the interaction between external problem representation and problem solving task. The mental representation for task solution is how the problem is represented in the working memory. When the types of information in the external problem representation match the characteristics of the problem-solving task, the problem solver formulates a mental representation that emphasize the same type of information, and the processes the problem solver uses to act on the mental representation of the problem will match the processes the problem solver uses to complete the task. The problem-solving process will be facilitated in terms of problem-solving effectiveness and efficiency, as there will be no need to transform the mental representation to accommodate the use of different processes to extract information from the external problem representation and to solve the problem.

**Diagrammatical Representation vs Sentential Representation**

Researchers have argued that "static pictures and diagrams are better than sentential representations" [34] in terms of information comprehension and inferencing. Two key factors distinguish diagrammatical representations from sentential representations in terms of cognition efficiency in human information processing systems - viz. information explicitness and search efficiency [35]. In terms of information explicitness, information represented in diagrams is more explicit than sentential representations and needs less computational effort [34]. In contrast, informationally equivalent representation of the same content but in a sentential form typically

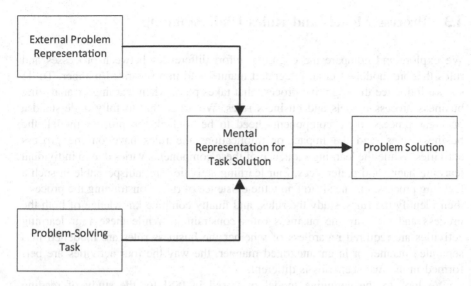

**Fig. 4.2.** Problem solving model

requires further mental formulation to make it explicit for use, which requires greater computational cognitive effort than for diagrammatical representation [34, 35]. In terms of search efficiency, in a diagrammatic representation, information is organized by location. Information elements that are relevant are grouped together, and information elements needed for inference are often present at adjacent locations, or connected with associations. Relations between graphical elements, map onto the relations of information elements in such a way that they restrict or enforce the kinds of interpretations that can be made [34]. This information grouping and connecting nature of diagrams, makes problem solving proceed through a smooth traversal of the diagram, in which little cognitive effort in terms of search computation is required [35]. In a sentential representation, information is often organized as a list of text items. Finding the relevant information item that matches the conditions of inferences requires searching linearly down the list, and the several items needed may be widely dispersed.

**Split-Attention Effect**
Information presented in an integrated manner is considered to reduce cognitive load, while split-source information can generate a heavy cognitive load in the process of information assimilation [97]. Accordingly, in the context of process and rule modelling, information representation research indicates that integrating business rules with relevant business process models can reduce cognitive load, thus improve the understanding of business processes. The processing of separate and mutually referring information, such as separate business rules and process models, frequently and unnecessarily requires attention to be split and switched between different sources, which inevitably consumes part of available working memory capacity and decreases cognitive resources available for learning [98, 99]. Thus, if information is integrated with the external representation, less cognitive effort is needed to assimilate information [32].

## 4.3   Process Models and Rules Understanding

We explore and compare the cognitive effort differences between processes and rules that are modelled in an integrated manner and in a separated manner. To do so, we introduce the cognitive process that takes place when learning or analyzing business process models and business rules. We argue that to fully understand a business process, three components need to be studied: the process model, the business rules, and the impact or implications the rules have on the process activities. While the learning sequence of these components varies due to individual learning habits and preferences, four learning activities are indispensable in such a learning process: one needs to know the existence of rules constraining the process, then identify the rules, study the rules, and finally combine knowledge of both the process and the way the business rules constrain it. While these four learning activities are required regardless of whether the business rules are modelled in a separated manner or in an integrated manner, the way the four activities are performed in the two scenarios is different.

We look to the cognitive model proposed in [88] for the study of reading comprehension process. The cognitive model proposed in [88] includes five stages, viz. goal formation, category selection, information extraction, integration, and recycling. We adapt this model to the business process and business rule context. Goal formation involves identification of the objective in the form of information that is to be found. In the context of business process and rule modelling, this is a rule awareness stage, which is the stage at which the user needs to become aware of the rules constraining a business activity. Category selection involves locating an appropriate category in which information could be relevant to the task. In our context, the focus is on each rule element/statement instead of a section of information, and we consider this to be a rule locating stage. Extraction of information relates to the extraction of useful information in the identified category so that the goal can be fulfilled. In our context, extraction alone is not sufficient and rule comprehension is required. Integration is the act of synthesizing the information extracted with previously obtained information. In our context, this stage relates to the synthesis of rules with process models. Recycling refers to transiting iteratively through the first four stages until the goal is fulfilled. In our context, it refers to the understanding of each business activity and the rules constraining it, thus the understanding of the overall business process with all relevant constraints. This stage is an iteration stage, which is crucial, but outside the scope of this research. Our process thus includes the stages of rule awareness, rule locating, rule comprehension, and information integration, as shown in Fig. 4.3. In the following sub-sections, we explore each stage of the process and the effect of integrated models versus separate representation.

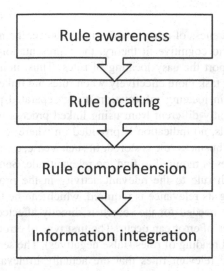

**Fig. 4.3.** Cognitive process in learning process models and rules

**Rule Awareness**

A prerequisite of a complete understanding of a business process is that a stakeholder must be aware of the existence of rules that the business activities are required to comply with. A lack of awareness of business rules can lead to non-compliant process execution, and can also result in longer times and costs in information system development. Representing business rules separately from process models doesn't fit the task of rule awareness. In a situation where the modelling is done in a separated manner, i.e. with a separate document listing business rules, there is a risk that the stakeholder's understanding of the underlying process model will be incomplete and problematic. Therefore, the execution of business activities by this stakeholder could breach policies or regulations, and generate exceptions that are not allowed by the rules. Further, such modelling might create problems at the requirement engineering phase of systems development projects. If there are rules that cannot be clearly identified, or if there is a lack of awareness of the rules, then these rules will be missed at the design and implementation stages, and, thus, could result in significant resource and time cost for remediation at later stages.

Researchers have found that the awareness of information is a basic human cognition feature if indications of relevance are explicitly provided [101], and diagrams, by their very nature, can explicitly connect relevant elements together [35]. Thus, we argue that awareness of business rules can be improved by integrating the rules with relevant process model diagrams through any of the already existing integration approaches. In particular, for very large and complex process models, we argue that integration methods such as hyperlinks of rules or collapsible annotations can improve rule awareness without increasing the complexity of the process model.

**Rule Locating**

After developing awareness of relevant rules in existence, the next step is to locate the rules. According to cognitive fit theory, the representation of process models and rules should support the easy locating of rules. Thus, individuals should perform the rule locating task more effectively when rules are linked to process model. The cognitive effort in locating information using separated process models and rules can be significantly different from using linked process models and rules.

In separated models, no indication is provided on where (e.g. location in a rule repository) a relevant business rule is stored. In such a case, a comprehensive search through all of the rules is required to find the relevant rule. Semantic interpretation and matching of each rule to the relevant activity in the process model for the purpose of identifying its relevance is required, which can be time-consuming and error-prone. The time needed for the search is directly affected by the size of the rule list, and two types of error can occur. The first type of error is missing relevant rules in the sequential reading of rules (false negatives). The second type of error is focusing on plausible relevant rules that are actually irrelevant (false positives), which results in additional cognitive load and could negatively affect the understanding of the process.

We argue that by integrating business rules with business process models, the cognitive effort in searching for relevant rules can be reduced. For example, the use of links [18] to integrate business rules with the models provides the location of relevant rules to the relevant part of the process. Representing business rules in annotations, and associating these with relevant activities that the rule constrains, can cognitive effort.

**Rule Comprehension**

Rule comprehension refers to the development of the understanding of an individual information element. A comprehension process takes place to assimilate the information after it is located. The argument that diagrams are better than sentential representations in terms of cognition efficiency has been well evaluated in research [34, 35]. Diagrammatic representations can explicitly represent information, making information readily available, while sentential descriptions typically are implicit and have to be mentally formulated [34], which requires greater cognitive effort.

Business rules can be represented using business process modelling languages as well as business rule modelling languages [17], or simply with natural language. Business process modelling languages generally have simple graphical syntax and semantics, while business rules languages are text-based and often abstract, and have a logical syntax that requires a degree of expertise for interpretation and modelling [25]. Although the representational capacity of process modelling languages may be lacking [5], as graphical information are easier to understand than sentential information [35], business rules that are integrated with business process models using graphical constructs, are easier to comprehend.

**Information Integration**

An individual business rule is unintelligible without the business process context. Implications of a business rule can only be correctly and fully interpreted when the context information is integrated. In other words, business activities cannot be fully understood until they are integrated with the constraining business rules. If information elements are not integrated physically in external representation, as is the case with separate business rules and process models, then one has to mentally integrate them, which imposes additional cognitive load [102].

The act of mental integration involves dividing attention between the multiple sources of information, cross-referencing each source, mentally manipulating diagrammatic and text elements, and finding relations among elements associated with the diagram and statements.

We argue that physical integration of business rules and process models can enhance process model comprehension and learning. By graphically modelling a rule in the relevant location on the process model, the cognitive load of dividing attention, cross-referencing, and integrating mental information of different information sources, is removed. Moreover, explicit relations between rules and activities in an integrated graphical representation, map onto the relations between the features of the process being modelled in such a way that they restrict or enforce the kinds of interpretations that can be made, which facilitates perceptual inferences [34].

## 4.4  Chapter Summary

In this chapter, we contribute to business process modelling research by providing a theoretical basis for exploring the effect of integrating business process models and business rules on the understanding of business processes. Our study introduces a 4-stage cognition process in the context of process and rule modelling, viz. developing awareness, locating, comprehending and integrating; and it adopts cognitive theories, including cognitive load theory, information representation theory, and information integration theory to explore each stage. The theoretical analysis indicates that the integration of business process models with business rules may improve awareness of business rules, reduce cognitive effort and reduce errors in the locating of business rules and the mental integration of business process models and business rules. Further, the integration of business rules and the diagrammatic form is more explicit for comprehension than sentential representation.

# Chapter 5
# The Effect of Rule Linking on Business Process Model Understanding

## 5.1 Overview

In this chapter, we develop hypotheses that rule linking can improve process model understanding accuracy, time efficiency, and reduce mental effort. Then we present our experiment investigating the effect of rule linking, a specific rule integration approach which uses graphical links to connect process model symbols with rules, on process model understanding. Our objective is two-fold. First, we test if linked rules can improve a model user's understanding of business process and rules. Second, by using eye-tracking technology in the experiment, we break down the statistics to the Process Model Area, Rule Area and Question Area and see what kind of information (process model, or rules) contributes most to our hypotheses. Third, we investigate the differences between other aspects of human cognitive behaviour such as single visit time and attention switching between groups, further exploring whether linked rules can improve process model understanding.

## 5.2 Hypotheses Development

The limitations of diagrammatic integration are widely known due to the expressibility limitations of process modelling languages [11]. Similarly, the drawbacks of rule integration through text annotations are duplication and potentially inconsistent rule representations [103]. Hence, in this study, we focus on a specific form of rule integration, namely link integration – an approach that points the model to the relevant rule, rather than duplicating that rule in the process model in either text or graphical form.

Link integration approaches incorporate visual links that connect the relevant rules to a section of the model – i.e. the links are explicitly represented in the activities or gateways that the rules constrain. This approach thus makes the connections of rules and corresponding activities explicit, presumably reducing cognitive load required to

© Springer Nature Switzerland AG 2019
W. Wang, *Integrating Business Process Models and Rules*, LNBIP 343,
https://doi.org/10.1007/978-3-030-11809-9_5

mentally connect rules to the appropriate part of the process model [104]. When rules are modelled in a separated manner, on the other hand, they have to be semantically interpreted and manually matched by the model user to the relevant parts of the model. This can be an error-prone process that requires the user to interpret the business rule against the background of the entire model to determine best fit. Accordingly, our first aim is to investigate the effect of link integration on process understanding accuracy, which means how well a process model is understood:

**Hypothesis 1:** Process models with linked rules are associated with better understanding accuracy compared to those with separated rules.

When rules are separated, all rules are organized as one set of rules, represented in some textual form (either plain text or in one of the business rule modelling languages). Lacking of connection of rules and process models, model users must intentionally be aware of rules when reading a process model, instead of naturally notice the rules by the hint of the link symbols when rules are integrated. Locating the relevant rules that constrain a specific activity or gateway requires a comprehensive search and semantic interpretation of the set (e.g. linearly down the entire list of rules), which takes more time to mentally connect the rules and the process model. Finally, separated models will take more mental effort in the information integration stage, as separated models makes it more difficult to cross-reference information from a process model and rules.

Accordingly, our second aim is to investigate the effect of rule linking on process understanding efficiency, focusing on how much time it takes a participant to review the process model and related rules to demonstrate understanding accuracy.

**Hypothesis 2:** Process models with linked rules are associated with better understanding time efficiency compared to those with separated rules.

As extra cognitive activities such as search and semantic interpretation are needed with rule linking, our third aim is to investigate the mental effort needed for understanding:

**Hypothesis 3:** Process models with linked rules are associated with less mental effort needed for understanding, than the models with separated rules.

Despite the benefits, link integration is not without limitations. First, people using linked rules may focus on the interactions of specific rules and process components, without a holistic understanding of the process model and rules as a prerequisite, thus may have an inaccurate understanding of process models and rules. Second, rule linking can cause attention switching [100], which means that users need to split their attention among multiple sources of information and mentally integrate them. Given separated rules as a whole list, one can choose to learn and assimilate more rules before switching attention to a process model, thus reducing the number of attention switches and time needed. It is therefore not clear to what extent the additional cognitive cost in terms of attention switching, counter-balances the improvement in understanding. Thus, a study is needed to investigate this effect of business process and rule integration. To this end, we propose an experimental approach to test our hypotheses.

## 5.3   Approach

In this section, first we introduce our experiment model. Then, we introduce the participants, materials, instruments and settings.

**Experiment Model**

We designed our experiment as a balanced single factor experiment with repeated measurement, based on an experiment design used to investigate the effects of process model decomposition on understanding [45]. This design is suitable to investigate the effects of one factor and allows us to analyse variations of a factor. The dependent variables are determined when the participants of the experiment apply factor levels to a particular object [45]. In our experiment, the use of linked rules is the considered factor, with factor levels "present" and "absent".

We have three main reasons to choose the within-subject design. First, we are using an eye-tracker in the experiment, which means only one participant can do the experiment at a time. Considering the time constraints, we can only hire a limited number of participants. A within-group design can increase the power of an experiment given the same number of participants as in a between-group design [105]. Second, the understanding quality of information largely depends on an individual's cognitive competence and experience. It is not feasible to accurately test the cognitive competence of participants and then allocate them to two groups of equal cognitive competence; nor were we allowed to collect any kind of GPA or class performance data. Thus, making the groups balanced is a challenge in a between-group design. Third, we want to increase the generalizability of the experiment by increasing domains, while controlling the learning effect.

The overall design is illustrated in Fig. 5.1. As shown in Fig. 5.1, the experiment includes two runs. Two process models, Model 1 and Model 2 with relevant rules for each process model will be used in each run, and each participant will be tested for all factor levels and all domains, thus (1) more data will be collected than from a single run experiment, (2) if one group is more competent in cognitive capacity, the group will do better in both factor levels, and (3) two domains are tested thus to increase the generalization ability of experiment results in terms of domains. Please note that the forms of rule representation are inversed in the two runs, as we should use same set of process model and rules, but different forms of rule representation between the two groups for each run. In the first run, Group 1 are given linked rules and Group 2 are given separated rules, while in the second run, Group 1 are given separated rules and Group 2 are given linked rules. Thus, we should expect inversed results in the two runs. For example, following Hypothesis 1, we should expect the answer correctness of Group 1 to be better than that of Group 2 in Model 1, but worse than that of Group 2 worse in Model 2.

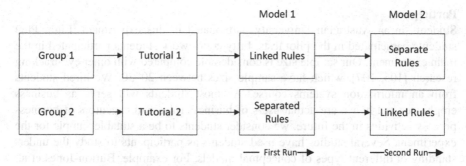

**Fig. 5.1.** Overall experiment approach

In our experiment, the use of linked rules is the considered factor, with factor levels "present" and "absent". As illustrated in Fig. 5.2, when linked rules are present, link buttons (labelled with "R") will be shown on activities and gateways in a process model. When a link button is clicked, the rules that are connected to the activity/gateway via the link button will be displayed on the "Relevant Rules" area on the right of the screen. When linked rules are absent, no link buttons will be shown in the process model, and all rules will be displayed on the "Relevant Rules" area on the right of the screen.

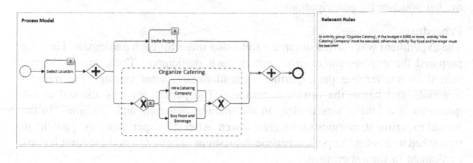

(a) Linked rules

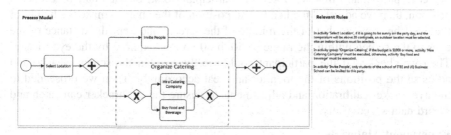

(b) Separated rules

**Fig. 5.2.** Independent variable illustration

**Participants**

Students in an Australian University participated in this experiment. Eight PhD students participated in the pilot tests. Fifty coursework students participated in the main experiment. Our sample size is considerable compared with other eye-tracking research [106, 107], which have sample sizes between 20–30. We hired students from an information systems course. As most students will serve as business employees and hence are actual users of business rules and executors of business process activities in the future, we consider students to be a suitable sample for the experiment. Several studies have used students as participants to study the understanding of different types of conceptual models. For example, Burton-Jones et al. [33] used novice students as participants to study the understanding of UML models, and Allen et al. [42] used students as participants to study the understanding of ER diagrams. In this study, all participants were required to have basic knowledge of typical conceptual models such as BPMN, flowcharts, UML or ER diagrams. We used BPMN as the process modelling language in the experiment as it is the de-facto process modelling language in practice, and many studies in business process models such as [45] and [46] use BPMN as the process modelling language. We only used the most basic BPMN symbols and easily understood conversational English language in the experiment materials, which don't need much experience to learn. As an incentive, each student was offered a $30 supermarket voucher for participation.

**Procedure**

The experiment was carried out in the following order for each participant. First, we prepared the experiment environment or each participant. Then, the participant started to answer the pre-experiment questionnaire, went through the training materials, and began the formal experiment. The participant was allowed to ask questions if anything was unclear in the training materials and examples. In the formal experiment, no questions were allowed. After the experiment, the participant was asked to answer the post-experiment questions. There was no time limit for any participant in the experiment.

**Preparation**

For each participant, first we asked the participant to sit on the chair in a relaxed position, then we adjusted the height and position of the chair to make the height of the eyes the same as that of the middle of the screen, and kept the distance of the eyes to the screen within the range of 50 to 80 cm, as required by the eye-tracker. Then we checked if the participant could see the text on the screen clearly, and adjusted the positions of the monitor and seat accordingly. Then we proceeded to the eye-tracker calibration and adjustments to ensure the eye-tracker can catch and record data successfully.

**Experiment Materials**

We describe each part of the materials below. The materials include a, pre-experiment questionnaire, a post-experiment questionnaire, a tutorial with examples, and the treatments. Appendix B includes the full experimental materials. A package of the entire experiment application is available for download on Dropbox[1].

## Questionnaire

Keeping the participants in different groups as similar as possible (balanced) is essential in between-group experiments. Unbalanced participants in different groups can cause the difference of results in an experiment, thus, whether such difference is caused by the treatment or by the difference between the participants in two groups is unknown, leading the experiment to a failure. We randomly allocated participants in two groups, and used two questionnaires to test if the two groups are balanced. The time to ask a participant a question should be carefully designed, as the answer of a question could be different before and after the experiment is carried out. For example, after participating the experiment, the answer of a question like the familiarity of process modelling could be increased, thus leads to bias. For the questions of which the answers could be affected by participating the experiment, such as the extent of familiarity of business process models and rules, the extent of familiarity of the knowledge domains used in the experiment, we put them into a pre-experiment questionnaire. To save a participant's mental effort before the experiment, objective questions which cannot be affected by the participation of the experiment, such as a participant's major and which year he or she is in, were put into a post-experiment questionnaire, together with a question asking participants which model consumed most of their mental effort in the experiment.

## Tutorial

The tutorial covered all BPMN elements and business rule concepts that participants would need to know to perform the tasks, e.g. activity, sequence, activity group, parallel gateway, exclusive gateway, and business rules. Sample process models, rules as well as questions and answers, are given during the tutorial. The instructions ask participants to study the process models, click the rule links, read the rules, and answer the questions. The order of treatments in tutorial and examples are consistent with the order in the experiment.

## Treatment Design

Learning effect means that participants are performing better in the late stages than in the early stages of an experiment, by gaining experience and knowledge about the experiment and the experiment designer's intention. Learning effect is a threat for successful experiments as it could lead to biased data and diminished difference of results between groups. To control the learning effect, two process models were used, and only three questions were asked for each process model. The information needed from a process model and rules to answer a question should be independent from each other thus the information learned from a previous question has little contribution to the current question.

---

[1]The experiment can be downloaded at: https://www.dropbox.com/s/g6jpb767m474vv2/experiment. rar?dl=0.

We designed process model 1 based on a space shuttle project management process model that was used to study the relationships of process model hierarchy [49] and process model understanding in [49, 108]. Then, we designed Model 2 following the complexity and structure of Model 1. The rules and questions of the two process models were designed in a manner to make them as close as possible. 3 rounds of pilot tests were conducted to make sure that the two sets of models, rules, and questions are at the same level in terms of complexity and difficulty. The rules covered common rule violations such as time constraint, route selection, and data logic.

Table 5.1 is a comparison of the material metrics in the two runs in detail. We adopted the basic metrics used to compare two process models such as number of activities, and number of arcs [45], metrics measuring the structure and complexity of control flow such as the number of parallel gateways and exclusive gateways, the number of branches in gateways, and the number of groups and activity groups as introduced in [109]. As the treatment also includes rules and questions, we also list the basic metrics for comparing the questions and rules in Table 5.1. As can be seen in Table 5.1, most of the metrics are the same, or close, in the two runs.

**Table 5.1.** Treatment comparison

| Metrics | | Model 1 | Model 2 |
|---|---|---|---|
| Process model | Activities | 16 | 15 |
| | Arcs | 34 | 33 |
| | Parallel gateways | 2 pairs | 2 pairs |
| | Parallel gateway branches[a] | 2, 3 | 2, 3 |
| | Exclusive gateways | 3 pairs | 3 pairs |
| | Exclusive gateway branches | 2, 2, 2 | 2, 2, 2 |
| | Cycles | 2 | 2 |
| | Starts | 1 | 1 |
| | Ends | 1 | 1 |
| | Activity groups | 3 (4, 4, 4) | 3 (2, 2, 3) |
| Rules | Rules count | 13 | 12 |
| | Words/characters | 303/1602 | 315/1595 |
| | Rule link count | 9 | 8 |
| | Rule groups[b] | $1 \times 6, 2 \times 2, 3 \times 1$ | $1 \times 5, 2 \times 2, 3 \times 1$ |
| Questions | Words/characters | 148/824 | 162/869 |
| Question 1 | Type | Path selection | Time constraint |
| | Words/characters | 43/207 | 52/310 |
| Question 2 | Type | Time constraint | Path selection |
| | Words/characters | 53/244 | 48/248 |
| Question 3 | Type | Calculation | Calculation |
| | Words/characters | 52/205 | 62/261 |

[a]A gateway can have several route branches. 2, 3 means the two gateways has 2 and 3 branches respectively.
[b]Rule group means how rules are grouped in rule links, with rule linking present. $1 \times 6$ means 6 rule links, each having one rule; $2 \times 2$ means 2 rule links, each having 2 rules; and $3 \times 1$ means 1 rule link, having 3 rules.

**Instruments and Settings**

The experiment was carried out in a lab. The pre-experiment and post-experiment questionnaires were implemented in Qualtrics[2]. The tutorial and experiment were implemented as an Eclipse RCP application[3]. The texts and diagrams were proved to be clearly visible from over 60 cm away in the pilot test. As shown in Fig. 5.3, the screen was divided into three Areas, viz. Process Model Area, Relevant Rules Area and Questions Area. As the recorded eye fixation positions would have inevitable offsets/errors from the actual positions in accordance with the level of accuracy of the eye-tracking system, we kept empty spaces between the contents of process model, rules, and questions to handle such errors. As shown in Fig. 5.4, some of the fixations recorded by the eye tracker in the Rules Area were out of the designed border of the Rule Area. Thus, the borders of the Process Model Area and Rule Area were adjusted accordingly as shown in Fig. 5.3. The complete process model and all the rules are displayed without the need for scrolling. No zooming is allowed in the application. All the texts and diagrams are in black and white so color blindness will not introduce bias to the experiment. We used Tobii Pro TX300, an eye tracker with a 23-inch screen of a resolution of $1920 \times 1080$ and capturing gaze data at 300 Hz[4]. The experiment was set in a lab. The lab has no window and the rooftop lights are the only light source. The materials, eye-tracker, and lights had the same settings for all participants.

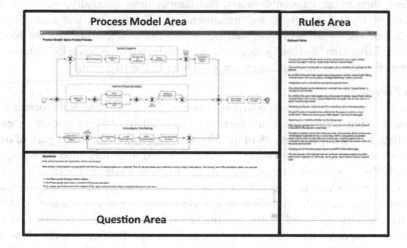

**Fig. 5.3.** Instrument illustration

---

[2]Qualtrics is a web-based survey platform. See: www.qualtrics.com.

[3]Eclipse RCP is a platform for building applications. See: https://wiki.eclipse.org/Rich_Client_Platform.

[4]For more specifications please see http://www.tobiipro.com/product-listing/tobii-pro-tx300.

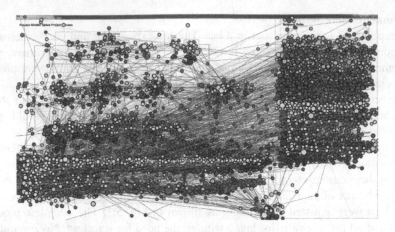

**Fig. 5.4.** Eye fixation illustration

## 5.4   Result Analysis

In this section, firstly we check if the two groups are balanced by comparing several types of variables, including identified gaze, process modelling familiarity, business rules familiarity, BPMN familiarity, domain familiarity, major, year, answer correctness, time spent, fixation duration, and tutorial time. Secondly, we check the validity of control variables and measurements. Thirdly, we test each of our hypotheses, and break down the statistics to the three Areas (the Process Model Area, the Rule Area, and the Question Area). Finally, we investigate the differences between single visit time and attention switching in the two groups.

**Data Screening**
Table 5.2 shows the group comparison statistics. Identified gaze is the percentage of eye tracking samples that are correctly identified by the eye tracker in each recording. In this experiment, 48 of the 50 recordings had an identified gaze of over 70%, while two outliers (in Group 1) had a 40% and 46% identified gaze respectively. In the experiment, two participants had to move closer to the display to see the text clearly, which is beyond the minimum distance required by the eye-tracker to identify gaze data. As identified gaze is the percentage of eye tracking samples that are correctly identified by the eye tracker, it is the indication of how well the eye-tracker captures data of a participant such as eye fixation counts. However identified gaze will not affect other metrics that are not captured by the eye-tracker. Thus, we discarded the two outliers in calculations of metrics that are captured by the eye tracker, such as fixation duration and visit count, and included them in the calculations of metrics that are not captured by the eye tracker, such as answer correctness and mental effort choices. BPM familiarity, rules familiarity, BPMN familiarity, Domain 1 familiarity, and Domain 2, were coded from 1–5, from most unfamiliar to most familiar. Major was coded as 0 and 1, where Information Technology, Computer Science, and Software Engineering were coded as 1; while

other non-CS or IS majors were coded as 0. Year means which year of a program a participant is in. 1 means the 1st year of a Bachelor program, while 5 means the 1st year of a Master's program. From Table 5.2 we can see that there were no significant differences between the two groups in most aspects.

**Table 5.2.** Group comparison

| Variable | Group | N | Mean | Std. dev | Skewness | Kurtosis | Test | p value |
|---|---|---|---|---|---|---|---|---|
| Identified gaze | G1 | 23 | 0.92 | 0.05 | −1.84 | 4.40 | Mann-Whitney | 0.812 |
| | G2 | 25 | 0.91 | 0.06 | −1.02 | 0.30 | | |
| BPM familiarity | G1 | 25 | 3.80 | 1.63 | 0.04 | −1.49 | t test | 0.611 |
| | G2 | 25 | 3.56 | 1.69 | 0.26 | −1.47 | | |
| Rules familiarity | G1 | 25 | 3.52 | 1.42 | 0.19 | −1.06 | t test | 0.768 |
| | G2 | 25 | 3.40 | 1.44 | 0.40 | −1.06 | | |
| BPMN familiarity | G1 | 25 | 2.36 | 1.32 | 1.75 | 3.24 | Mann-Whitney | 0. 557 |
| | G2 | 25 | 2.16 | 1.11 | 2.07 | 5.52 | | |
| Domain 1 familiarity | G1 | 25 | 2.48 | 1.33 | 1.91 | 4.94 | Mann-Whitney | 0. 617 |
| | G2 | 25 | 2.76 | 1.48 | 1.04 | 0.06 | | |
| Domain 2 familiarity | G1 | 25 | 2.68 | 1.31 | 0.77 | −0.69 | t test | 0.101 |
| | G2 | 25 | 3.36 | 1.55 | 0.01 | −1.38 | | |
| Major | G1 | 25 | 0.60 | 0.50 | −0.44 | −1.98 | t test | 0.766 |
| | G2 | 25 | 0.64 | 0.49 | −0.62 | −1.76 | | |
| Year | G1 | 25 | 3.88 | 1.67 | −0.97 | −0.65 | t test | 0.726 |
| | G2 | 25 | 3.72 | 1.54 | −0.38 | −1.16 | | |
| Answer correctness | G1 | 25 | 0.68 | 0.25 | −0.71 | −0.26 | t test | 0.675 |
| | G2 | 25 | 0.70 | 0.19 | −1.20 | 1.90 | | |
| Time | G1 | 23 | 837.33 | 262.12 | 1.02 | 1.75 | t test | 0.808 |
| | G2 | 25 | 851.64 | 313.52 | 1.01 | 0.52 | | |
| Fixation duration | G1 | 23 | 732.67 | 242.51 | 1.14 | 1.98 | t test | 0.959 |
| | G2 | 25 | 729.96 | 272.40 | 1.11 | 0.89 | | |
| Tutorial time | G1 | 23 | 587.37 | 223.47 | 0.31 | −0.81 | t test | 0.562 |
| | G2 | 25 | 550.56 | 213.60 | 0.56 | −0.73 | | |

**Tests of Hypotheses**

For each dependent variable, we first checked if the dependent variable could be assumed to be normally distributed. Following [45], we considered a variable to be normally distributed if the standardized skewness and standardized kurtosis were within the range of [−2, 2]. If data from both groups were normally distributed, we checked whether the data met the assumption of equal variance using dependent Levene's test[5] at the significance level of 0.05, and then used the independent-sample

---

[5]Levene's test is an inferential statistic used to assess the equality of variances for a variable calculated for two or more groups.

t test. If data in any group were not normally distributed, we used the Mann-Whitney U test[6] across groups. Significance level means the risk that we accept a hypothesis while the hypothesis is actually wrong, and a p value corresponds to the significance level. For example, a p value of 0.03 corresponds to a significance level of 0.03, meaning that the risk of accepting a hypothesis, which is actually wrong, is 3%. Conventionally, 0.1, 0.05, and 0.001 are used as significance levels, and larger significance levels are used with smaller sample sizes [110]. As we have a small sample size in our experiment, we consider a significance level below 0.01 is strongly supporting a hypothesis, a significance level between 0.01 and 0.005 is supporting a hypothesis, and a significance level between 0.05 and 0.1 is also supporting a hypothesis, although the support is weaker, as the possibility of accepting the hypothesis which is actually right is at least 90%. Following the suggestion of reporting actual significance levels in [110], we report the actually significance level of each hypothesis test. We describe the results for each hypothesis in turn.

For Hypothesis 1, the correctness of question answers was normally distributed, and the data met the assumption of equal variance (p value of Levene's test is 0.61 for Model 1 and 0.25 for Model 2). We therefore ran independent-sample t tests between Group 1 and Group 2, with the correctness of answers as the dependent variable, for the two models separately.

Table 5.3 shows the results. The p value of answer correctness between groups in Model 1 is 0.088, indicating a significance level below 0.1 but above 0.05. Thus Hypothesis 1 is weakly supported in Model 1. The p value of answer correctness between groups in Model 2 is 0.042, indicating a significance level below 0.05, which means Hypothesis 2 is supported in Model 2.

**Table 5.3.** Test of Hypotheses 1 – understanding accuracy

|                        | Group | N  | Mean | Std. dev | t     | p (1-tailed) |
|------------------------|-------|----|------|----------|-------|--------------|
| Correctness in Model 1 | G1    | 25 | .73  | .25      | 1.37  | 0.088        |
|                        | G2    | 25 | .63  | .29      |       |              |
| Correctness in Model 2 | G1    | 25 | .63  | .36      | −1.77 | 0.042        |
|                        | G2    | 25 | .79  | .27      |       |              |

**Conclusion 1:** Hypothesis 1 (Process models with linked rules are associated with better understanding accuracy compared to those with separated rules) is weakly supported in Model 1, and supported in Model 2.

For Hypothesis 2, the time spent by group 2 in Model 2 was not normally distributed. We ran independent-sample Mann-Whitney tests between Group 1 and Group 2, with the time (from beginning to the end of answering the last question in each run) as the dependent variable. The test result of Hypothesis 2 is shown in

---

[6]The Mann-Whitney U test is used to compare differences between two independent groups when the dependent variable is not normally distributed.

Table 5.4. Table 5.4 shows that the p value of time used between groups in Model 1 is 0.015, indicating a significance level between 0.01 and 0.05. Thus Hypothesis 2 is supported in Model 1. The p value of time used between groups in Model 2 is 0.009, indicating a significance level below 0.01. Thus Hypothesis 2 is strongly supported in Model 2.

**Table 5.4.** Test of Hypothesis 2: understanding efficiency

|  | Group | N | Mean | Std. dev | p (1-tailed) |
|---|---|---|---|---|---|
| Time used in Model 1 | G1 | 23 | 368.76 | 110.23 | 0.015 |
|  | G2 | 25 | 481.18 | 218.10 |  |
| Time used in Model 2 | G1 | 23 | 468.57 | 173.06 | 0.009 |
|  | G2 | 25 | 370.46 | 116.88 |  |

**Conclusion 2:** Hypothesis 2 (Process models with linked rules are associated with better understanding time efficiency compared to those with separated rules) is supported in Model 1, and strongly supported in Model 2.

We used both an objective measurement (fixation durations) and a subjective measurement (a subjective question about which model takes more mental effort) to test Hypothesis 3. For the objective measurement of Hypothesis 3, the eye-fixation durations in the two runs were not normally distributed. We therefore ran independent-sample Mann-Whitney tests for the two runs separately. The objective test of Hypothesis 3 is shown in Table 5.5. From Table 5.5 we can see that the p value of fixation duration between groups in Model 1 is 0.024, indicating a significance level between 0.01 and 0.05. Thus Hypothesis 3 is supported in Model 1. The p value of fixation durations between groups in Model 2 is 0.007, indicating a significance level below 0.01. Thus Hypothesis 3 is strongly supported in Model 2.

**Table 5.5.** Test of Hypothesis 3: objective mental effort

|  | Group | N | Mean | Std. dev | p (1-tailed) |
|---|---|---|---|---|---|
| Fixation duration in Model 1 | G1 | 23 | 322.98 | 100.30 | 0.024 |
|  | G2 | 25 | 411.43 | 188.22 |  |
| Fixation duration in Model 2 | G1 | 23 | 409.68 | 159.94 | 0.007 |
|  | G2 | 25 | 318.53 | 102.31 |  |

**Conclusion 3a:** Hypothesis 3 (Process models with linked rules are associated with less mental effort needed for understanding, than the models with separated rules) is supported in Model 1, and strongly supported in Model 2, in the objective measurement.

For the subjective measurement of Hypothesis 3, the results of the perception of mental effort are shown in Table 5.6. In Group 1, 0 participants selected Model 1 (linked rules), while 23 participants selected Model 2 (separated rules) as the model requiring the *more* mental effort. Two participants selected '*equal*' as the answer. In Group 2, 11 participants selected Model 1 (separated rules), while 6 participants selected Model 2 (linked rules) as the model requiring *more* mental effort. Eight participants selected '*equal*' as the answer. From Table 5.6, we can intuitively see that participants indicate that models with separated rules require more mental effort, regardless of model content (Model 1 or Model 2).

**Table 5.6.** Subjective mental effort

|  | Group 1 | Group 2 |
|---|---|---|
| Model 1 costs more mental effort | 0 (linked rules) | 11 (separated rules) |
| Model 2 costs more mental effort | 23 (separated rules) | 6 (linked rules) |
| Equal | 2 | 8 |

To statistically compare linked and separated rules, we coded the perception answers as follows: When a model with linked rules was selected as the model that required more mental effort, linked rules were assigned two points. When the model with separated rules was selected as the model that required more mental effort, separated rules were assigned two points. When a participant selected the two models as equal, both linked rules and separated rules were assigned one point. We used a *t test* for the difference in average mental effort perception between linked and separated rules. Table 5.7 shows that subjective mental effort between the two rule modelling methods is 0.000, corresponding to a significance level of 0.000. Thus, Hypothesis 3 is strongly supported in the subjective measurements.

**Table 5.7.** Coded subjective mental effort

|  | N | Coded mean | Std. dev | p (1-tailed) |
|---|---|---|---|---|
| Linked rules | 50 | 0.44 | 0.70 | 0.000 |
| Separated rules | 50 | 1.56 | 0.70 |  |

**Conclusion 3b:** Hypothesis 3 (Process models with linked rules are associated with less mental effort needed for understanding, than the models with separated rules) is strong supported in the subjective measurement.

**Single Visit Time**
Besides the 3 hypotheses, we are also interested in other metrics that may result from linked rules. Single visit time is defined as the time interval between the first fixation on one area and the end of the last fixation within the same area where there have been no fixations outside the Area. With linked rules, only a few rules will be displayed in the Rules Area, while with separated rules, all rules will be displayed in the Rules Area, which allows a participant to spend more time to read more rules before switching his or her attention to other areas. Intuitively, we speculated that single visit time, given separated rules, could be longer than that given for linked

rules. As shown in Fig. 5.5, the group that were given linked rules have shorter single visit times in each run. Mann-Whitney test results in Table 5.8 show that the p value of single visit time between groups is 0.070 in Model 1, indicating a difference. The p values of single visit time between groups is 0.003 in Model 2, indicating a strong difference.

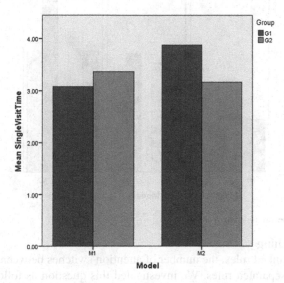

**Fig. 5.5.** Single visit time

**Table 5.8.** Single visit time comparison

| | Group | N | Mean | Std. dev | p (1-tailed) |
|---|---|---|---|---|---|
| Single visit time in Model 1 | Group 1 | 23 | 3.08 | 1.02 | 0.070 |
| | Group 2 | 25 | 3.37 | 0.74 | |
| Single visit time in Model 2 | Group 1 | 23 | 3.87 | 1.02 | 0.003 |
| | Group 2 | 25 | 3.16 | 0.89 | |

To further investigate the reason of such difference, we broke down the single visit time in to the three Areas, i.e. the Process Model Area, the Rule Area, and the Question Area. From Fig. 5.6 we can intuitively see that the difference between the two groups in single visit time was mainly caused by the single visit time difference in the Rules Area, while the differences between single visit time in the Model Area and the Question Area are close. This implicates that using linked rules, a participant can find the needed information in an area faster than using separated rules.

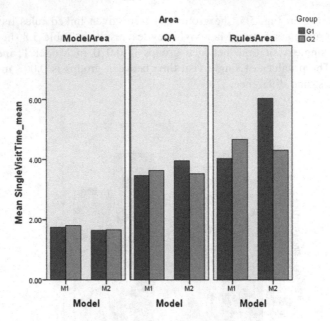

**Fig. 5.6.** Visit time breakdown

## Attention Switching

With respect to linked rules, the number of attention switches between areas may be higher than for separated rules. We investigated this question as follows. First, we compared the sum up of the number of visits to each area of each group (a visit to an area implies that the attention is switched from another area to this area). Then, we compared the number of attention switches in the three areas in pairs (Fig. 5.7).

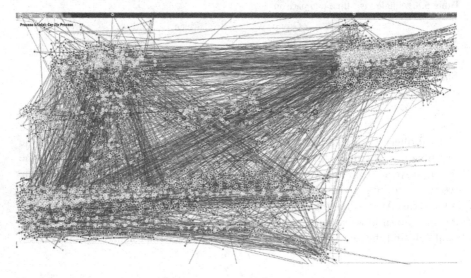

**Fig. 5.7.** Attention switching illustration

From Fig. 5.8, we can see that the overall number of attention switches given linked rules are slightly smaller than given separated rules. The Mann-Whitney tests in Table 5.9 show that the two groups were not significantly different in either run.

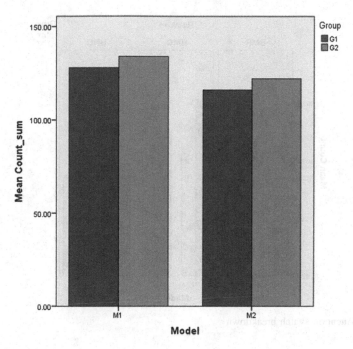

**Fig. 5.8.** Sum of visits

**Table 5.9.** Mann-Whitney tests of visit count

| Model | Group | N | Mean | Std. dev | p (1-tailed) |
|---|---|---|---|---|---|
| Visit count sum in Model 1 | Group 1 | 23 | 190.43 | 83.94 | 0.296 |
| | Group 2 | 25 | 199.52 | 86.50 | |
| Visit count sum in Model 2 | Group 1 | 23 | 180.22 | 92.86 | 0.214 |
| | Group 2 | 25 | 183.64 | 73.85 | |

Figure 5.9 shows the number of attention switches in the three areas in pairs. As we can see from the figure, compared with the group that was given separated rules, the group that was given linked rules, had more attention switches between the Model Area and the Question Area, had fewer attention switches between the Rules Area and the Question Area, and had more attention switches between the Model Area and the Rules Area. Figure 5.10 illustrates the difference in attention switch counts between linked rules and separated rules in both runs. Compared with separated rules, given linked rules, participants spent 14% more attention switching

between process models and rules, 18% more attention switches between process models and questions, and 26% less attention switches between questions and rules than for the linked rules.

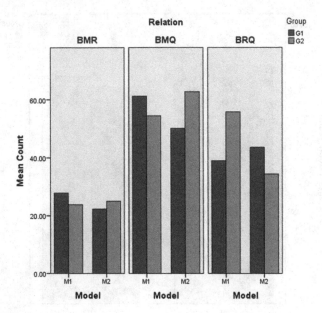

**Fig. 5.9.** Attention switch breakdown

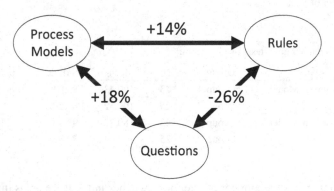

**Fig. 5.10.** Attention switch count difference between groups

As attention switching is an indication of mentally integrating information from two separated sources [97], and more attention switches indicates a stronger mental information integration activity, we can infer that compared with the group that was given linked rules, the group that was given separated rules had less mental information integration activity between the process models and rules, and had more information integration activity between process models and questions, while it had less information integration activity between rules and questions. We can further infer that due to the lack of mental information integration between rules and process models, the group that was given separated rules, had a worse understanding of the connection between rules and process models. The group tried to answer the questions merely from information in the rules, without using enough information from process models, and the connections between rules and process models. This attention switching difference could be a possible cause of the lower understanding quality in the group.

Due to the lack of information integration between rules and process models, the group given separated rules had a weaker understanding of the connection between rules and process models. Also, the group given separated rules relied too much on information from rules to answer questions, without using enough information from process models. These are the two causes of a lower understanding quality.

## 5.5   Chapter Summary

In this chapter, the study aimed to determine the effect that linked rules can have on user understanding of a business process model. We focused on three aspects of understanding: accuracy, time efficiency, and mental effort. Our experiment results showed that all the three hypotheses are supported. Second, we found that while rule links can reduce time spent per visit overall, which is mainly caused by the reduction of time spent per visit in the Rules Area, it will not increase the overall number of attention switches in the three areas. Instead, rule links can increase visits to the Process Model Area while decreasing visits to the Rules Area.

# Chapter 6
# Identification of Factors Affecting Business Process and Business Rule Integration

## 6.1 Overview

In this chapter, we present the identification and evaluation of factors that can affect the decision of whether or not to integrate business process modelling and business rule modelling. First we present the methodology for factor identification, evaluation and decision analysis. Then we present the factors, followed by the empirical evaluation. Finally, we provide six guidelines based on the data analysis from the evaluation.

## 6.2 Approach

We carried out a systematic process of identification of factors that are thought to influence the decision about whether to model business rules in an integrated or separated manner [111]. To identify these factors, a systematic literature review was conducted based on a comprehensive set of well-regarded Information Systems and Computer Science journals and conferences published between 1990–2013, a period of time after the initial proposal of the integration of the two approaches [76]. Our data set consisted of over 43,000 full-text articles (see Table 6.1). Each article was inspected and prepared (with OCR) for a full text search. Subsequently, a full-text search was conducted using the search term "business rule". We regarded a paper as relevant if the term "business rule" occurred three or more times within the body of the text and only selected the papers that met this criterion for the next round of analysis. Two hundred and fifty-five papers were identified following this step.

For each of the papers, we read the abstract, the introduction to the paper, and each paragraph where the term "rule" occurred to determine if the paper was relevant to our purpose. A paper was identified as relevant if a characteristic of a

© Springer Nature Switzerland AG 2019
W. Wang, *Integrating Business Process Models and Rules*, LNBIP 343,
https://doi.org/10.1007/978-3-030-11809-9_6

**Table 6.1.** Data set of 1990–2013 publications

| Type | Acronym | # papers | # relevant papers |
|---|---|---|---|
| Conferences | ACIS, AMCIS, CAiSE, ECIS, ER, HICSS, ICIQ, ICIS, IFIP, IRMA, IS Foundations, PACIS, BPM, WIDM, WISE, CIKM, SIGIR, VLDB | 27,326 | 29 |
| Journals | BPMJ, CAIS, EJIS, I&M, ISF, ISJ (Black-well), ISJ (Sarasota), JAIS, ISR, MISQ, MISQ Executive, TKDE, DKE, CACM, DSS, TOIS | 15,695 | 49 |

business rule such as change frequency, reusability or impact, for example, was mentioned or discussed in the paper. Seventy-eight papers were identified in this step.

The set of 78 relevant papers was then read in full and manually coded with a dedicated coding protocol. The coding protocol was refined and agreed to by the three researchers after an initial coding of five articles to define the initial protocol. The final protocol contained the title of the paper, context, factor name, and refinement.

One researcher carried out the initial coding exercise through iterative coding of relevant sentences of each identified paper as contexts in the spreadsheet, and selecting representative keywords as possible factor names. Then three researchers worked together to refine the result. The refinement followed these steps: (1) Read each context and check if the selected keywords can truly represent the corresponding paragraph context, and change for better keywords when necessary. (2) Cluster similar keywords semantically into clusters. (3) Select a representative label for each cluster and clarify its definition. The results were refined over three iterations until all three researchers were satisfied with the selection and definition of each factor. Twelve factors were identified in total through this process.

Table 6.2 exemplifies how the coding and refinement were carried out in this study. In Table 6.2, keywords *Validity Checking* and *Checking Responsibility* are clustered together, and *Governance Responsibility* is selected as a representative label for this cluster. Keywords *Stability, Changes,* and *change* are clustered together, and *Rate of Change* is selected as a representative label for this cluster.

To validate the identified factors, and to evaluate their relative importance and effects on the decision as to whether a business rule is modelled independently or modelled in a business process model, and when they should remain separate, we designed a survey. The target participants of the empirical evaluation were the authors of the papers that were the sources for the factor identification. These academics were invited to participate in an online survey hosted on Qualtrics[1].

The survey begins with background introduction and demographic questions. Then for each factor, the survey first gives a definition and description of the factor, then asks a participant the importance of the factor using a 1–7 Likert question. If

---

[1]Qualtrics is a web-based survey platform. See: www.qualtrics.com.

**Table 6.2.** Example of coding and refinement snippet

| Source title | Context | Keywords (Factor name) | Refinement |
|---|---|---|---|
| From the stone age to the cloud: a case study of risk-focused process improvement | "The problem of rule checking by embedded programs is that (1) rules handled by programs are limited to simple ones; comprehension of complex rules are left for humans." | Checking Responsibility | Cluster as Governance Responsibility |
| A process model for analyzing and managing flexibility in information systems | "As a best practice, the project team determined that if the rule is likely to change in the future (based on past experience), the rules should go in the rule engine or in data tables accessible by the business user. If the rules rarely change, it is more likely to stay in the process model only." | Change | Cluster as Rate of Change |

the answer is 1 or 2, the participant will be asked about the reason for the selection and then the participant will go to the next factor. If the answer is within 3 to 7, then the survey asks a participant that given two opposite values of the factor, whether a business rule should be integrated with a process model or not. For example, for the factor Rate of Change, the question will be "Considering the factor Rate of Change being frequent or infrequent, where do you think a business rule should be modelled respectively". After the questions for each factor, the survey asks a participant to rank the factors, and suggest factors that are missing in the survey. Figure 6.1 is a screenshot of questions about the factor Rate of Change in the survey, and the full survey is in Appendix A.

The survey was pilot-tested and revised through two rounds. In the first iteration, three Ph.D. students were asked to complete the survey and give feedback. Then the revised survey was pilot-tested with two Ph.D. students and a Master's student, and an international expert in requirements modelling. The revisions included changes to the factor definitions and questions to improve clarity. Randomization of questions was introduced as well.

Invitations were sent to 112 authors of the 78 papers and 35 responses were received, of which 13 were removed later due to data incompleteness. Thus, 22 usable responses were received in total, representing a response rate of 23.08% when calculated as responses per paper. Since it is hard to achieve a high response rate in such empirical research [112], a response rate of approximately 20% is generally considered to be usable [113, 114].

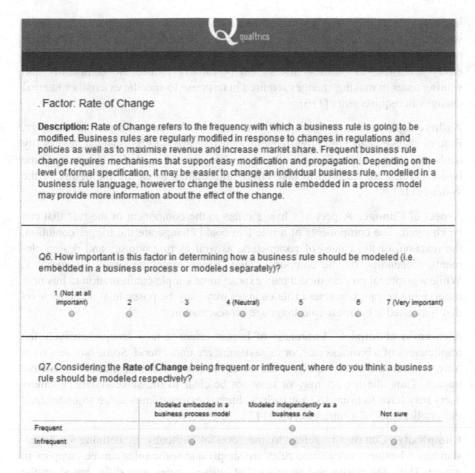

**Fig. 6.1.** Survey screenshot

## 6.3 Business Rule Modelling Factors

In total, we identified twelve factors in the first phase of our study. In the following, a summary of the definition of each factor is provided, with arguments collected from the literature review. Only the definition parts, i.e., texts in *italics* are used in the survey. The argument and examples are excluded to limit possible introduction of bias to the responses.

**Accessibility.** Accessibility refers to the user's need to view and manipulate a business rule. If a stakeholder can easily view or manipulate a rule in a format that is suitable to his or her need, then the rule has high accessibility, otherwise, the rule has low accessibility. Making business rule repositories accessible to stakeholders whenever required, as well as in a format that is suitable to their needs, is a basic requirement of information systems [115]. Separating the rules can make rules easily accessible to business users, and potentially reduce the complexity and waiting times in making changes required in response to specific external or internal changes in requirements [116].

**Agility.** Agility refers to how quickly a business rule can be adapted to a change. Rate of change deals with how frequently the rule needs to be changed, and agility deals with how long will it take for each change to be modelled in a rule. Some business rules are required to take effect immediately to ensure the agility of the system [116].

**Aspect of Change.** Aspect of Change refers to the component of the rule that can be changed. The components of a rule that could change are the trigger condition, the reaction, or the values of parameters, as well as rule phrases and design elements. Depending on the component, the change might be simple or complex. While a graphical process model may expose some simple configuration to business users, more complex business rule changes may only be possible at a deeper level that may need a business rule language representation.

**Awareness of Impact.** Awareness of Impact refers to how comprehensively the implications of a business rule, or its revisions, are understood. Some business rules have a direct and clear impact, while other rules may have an indirect or unclear impact. Thus, the impact may or may not be clear to the stakeholders. Business users may have to bring to bear their additional external knowledge to understand the implications of a business rule [117].

**Complexity.** Complexity refers to the level of difficulty in defining or understanding a business rule. Some rules are simple and some rules can be complex in nature. Thus, the clarity and simplicity of business rules may differ based on the chosen representation [25]. Certain kinds of business rules cannot be clearly expressed in a business process modelling language due to language representation limitations, while others may be easily modelled as a standalone rule due to the more precise representation capability [118].

**Criticality.** Criticality refers to the importance of the rule. Violation of critical rules can lead to severe consequences for the organization, while a violation of non-critical rules may be less severe. Integrating a business rule with a business process model can ensure that the business rule is implemented enterprise-wide.

**Governance Responsibility.** Governance Responsibility refers to who ensures that business activities are in accordance with business rules. Rules can be governed automatically by programs/systems, or manually by humans [119]. If the business rule is to be checked automatically in the system, machine readability and execution will be a basic requirement, while context availability and user-friendly representation will be more important if the rule is to be checked by a human.

**Implementation Responsibility.** Implementation Responsibility refers to who is charged with implementing or updating the business rule. Both business users and technical users could be responsible for the implementation of a business rule. Business users generally have the configuration responsibility over business rules in business rule repositories [8] and may not have process modelling expertise, whereas technical staff or the IT department may be responsible for the implementation of business processes.

**Rate of Change.** Rate of Change refers to the frequency at which a business rule requires modification. Business rules can change in response to changes in regulations and policies. Frequent business rule change requires mechanisms that support easy modification and propagation. It is possible that frequently changed business rules could be modelled in a stand-alone fashion, rather than being integrated with graphical process models where they could be labor-intensive and cumbersome to update [120].

**Reusability.** Reusability refers to the potential for a rule to be used in new contexts. An existing business rule may be adapted or modified to fit new contexts and scenarios to reduce the resources required in developing new rules. Scattered [118] and duplicated [103] rules make it difficult to evaluate and maintain integrity and consistency [121]. If a reusable business rule is integrated with a business process model, the development, testing, and maintenance efforts may be increased when that rule changes and requires updating [103, 122].

**Rule Source.** Rule Source refers to the origin of the business rule. Rule sources could be external or internal – e.g. laws and regulations or internal policies and standards. Requirements defined by external regulatory bodies can be "critical to the organization, while being outside the scope of their control. Particularly when the changes pertain to compliance with regulations" [8].

**Scope of Impact.** Scope of Impact refers to the breadth of the impact of the rule. The impact of a business rule can be focused on an activity, an entire process, a department or the entire organization [8]. If an organization-wide business rule is integrated with a large number of business process models, any update to the rule will lead to a change in a large number of models, thus triggering re-work and risk of inconsistency [2, 8].

The factors and papers where each factor was identified from is listed in Table 6.3.

**Table 6.3.** Factors and sources

| Factor | Relevant works |
|---|---|
| Accessibility | [103, 115, 116, 123, 124] |
| Agility | [103, 116, 119, 121, 123, 125–133] |
| Aspect of Change | [103, 121] |
| Awareness of Impact | [103, 117, 127] |
| Complexity | [6, 103, 118, 122, 122, 123, 127, 134–141] |
| Criticality | [121, 142–146] |
| Governance Responsibility | [119, 131, 147–149] |
| Implementation Responsibility | [134, 150] |
| Rate of Change | [120–123, 125, 128, 131, 134, 145, 151–161] |
| Reusability | [103, 118, 119, 121, 121, 122, 124, 143, 152, 162, 163] |
| Rule Source | [8, 164] |
| Scope of Impact | [134, 150] |

## 6.4   Empirical Validation of Factors

In this section, we present the validation and empirical evaluation of these twelve factors. The main aim of the empirical study was to derive a factor ranking from the perceived importance by experts, and to analyse expert suggestions as to how these factors are affecting the modelling rules in practice. In the following, first we present a discussion on the factors' importance rankings, and then investigate the indications of how these factors are affecting the modelling of rules.

**Demographics**

The participants of our survey were academics and practitioners who authored the papers relevant to this study. Demographics are shown in Table 6.4. The overall process modelling experience of participants in our study is higher than in other similar studies, e.g. [6]. However, compared with experience of process modelling, the experience of rule modelling is slightly lower, which is an indication that fewer participants are familiar with rule modelling.

**Table 6.4.** Participant demographics

| Variable | Values | % |
|---|---|---|
| Responses | 22 | 23% |
| Academics | 20 | 91% |
| Practitioners | 2 | 9% |
| Process modelling notations used | 1 | 9% |
| | 2 | 32% |
| | 3 | 14% |
| | 4 | 14% |
| | 5 | 18% |
| | >5 | 14% |

(continued)

**Table 6.4.** (continued)

| Variable | Values | % |
|---|---|---|
| Rule modelling notations used | 0 | 23% |
| | 1 | 14% |
| | 2 | 27% |
| | 3 | 23% |
| | 4 | 9% |
| | 5 | 5% |
| Experience in process modelling overall | <2 years | 14% |
| | 2–5 years | 18% |
| | 5–10 years | 18% |
| | >10 years | 50% |
| Experience in rule modelling notations overall | None | 14% |
| | <2 years | 9% |
| | 2–5 years | 27% |
| | 5–10 years | 27% |
| | >10 years | 23% |
| Process models created | <10 | 18% |
| | 10–25 | 41% |
| | 25–50 | 9% |
| | >50 | 32% |

**Factor Importance**

To distinguish the importance of each factor, we asked each participant to select the five most important factors and rank the selected factors by importance. As current top-k ranking algorithms require k to be a constant across all rankings [165], only the top-5 factors were used in the ranking and agreement analysis. We note that while three participants selected 6, 7, and 7 factors respectively, these factors are already in top 50% of factors by importance (see Table 6.5).

**Table 6.5.** Aggregated ranking using Borda's method

| Factor | Total points | Rank | Std. deviation |
|---|---|---|---|
| Agility | 42 | 1 | 2.05 |
| Criticality | 41 | 2 | 2.19 |
| Rate of Change | 37 | 3 | 2.00 |
| Reusability | 37 | 4 | 1.87 |
| Accessibility | 32 | 5 | 1.79 |
| Awareness of Impact | 27 | 6 | 1.73 |
| Complexity | 25 | 7 | 1.16 |
| Governance Responsibility | 21 | 8 | 1.61 |
| Scope of Impact | 17 | 9 | 1.79 |
| Aspect of Change | 9 | 10 | 1.05 |
| Implementation Responsibility | 9 | 11 | 1.39 |
| Rule Source | 2 | 12 | 0.31 |

To calculate ranking consensus between the participants, the rankings provided by each participant were aggregated into a single ranking. Consensus ranking [166] is adopted as it can minimize the overall distances between all rankings. We adopted the classical Borda's method [167] to calculate the aggregated ranking, which is commonly used in literature [166].

Following this method, a factor which was ranked $i \leq 5$ in an individual ranking was assigned 5-$i$ points. A factor which was not in the top-5 was assigned 0 points. The total points assigned to each factor are the sum of the factor's points in each individual ranking.

As shown in Table 6.5, the most important factor is *agility*, and *criticality* is a close second. *Rate of change* and *reusability* are jointly ranked third. *Accessibility*, *awareness* of *impact*, *complexity*, *governance responsibility* and *scope of impact* follow in that order. The lowest ranked factors are *aspect of change*, *implementation responsibility*, and *rule source*.

While Borda's method allows us to aggregate the ranking, the level of agreement between experts' individual rankings is an important question. If no agreement was reached, the aggregated ranking is meaningless. We use *compactness* [168], to calculate the degree of agreement, following the method in [169].

$$compactness = \sqrt{\frac{\sum_{i=1}^{m} \sum_{j=1}^{m} (r_i - r_j)^2}{m(m-1)}} \qquad (1)$$

Normalized compactness ranges from 0 to 1, where 0 means the ranking lists are identical (i.e. participants agree with each other) while 1 means the ranking lists are completely different. In formula (1), $m$ is the number of factors, $r_i - r_j$ is the distance between rankings $r_i$ and $r_j$. We adopt the commonly used Kendall's tao method [170] to calculate $r_i - r_j$. Kendall's tao distance is calculated using formula (2). $x, y$ are elements in the set P which consists of elements in rankings $r_i$ and $r_j$. $p$ is assigned ½ as the neutral approach. The detailed algorithm is described in [170].

$$r_i - r_j = \sum_{\{x,y\} \in P(r_i, r_j)} \bar{K}_{i,j}^{(p)}(r_i, r_j) \qquad (2)$$

Following formulae (1) and (2), the compactness of all the rankings is 0.36, and the degree of agreement among the participants is 0.64, which is deemed acceptable [169]. Table 6.5 also shows the standard deviation for each factor to provide an indication of the level of agreement on a single factor.

## 6.5   Business Rule Embedding Guidelines

While the ranking in the first part of our analysis provides an indication as to which factors should be considered, it does not provide any guidance as to how a rule should be modelled. To carry out such an analysis we must first determine which factors have consistent responses from participants, in terms of their effect on rule modelling. Thus, we first distinguish "affecting" factors from "non-affecting" factors. A factor is non-affecting if there is no significant difference in expert opinion as to how that factor affects modelling. For example, in Table 6.6, for factor *aspect of change*, experts were asked to indicate if the rule (to be changed or added) should be modelled in an integrated manner or modelled separately, given the aspect of the rule change to be simple and complex respectively.

**Table 6.6.** Vote distributions for non-affecting factors (When a participant indicated that a factor is not important (importance rated as 1 or 2), this question was not applicable (N/A).)

| Factor | Value | Integrate | Separate | Other |
|---|---|---|---|---|
| Aspect of Change | High | 4 | 11 | 3 |
| | Low | 4 | 11 | 3 |
| Awareness of Impact | Frequent | 3 | 11 | 4 |
| | Infrequent | 5 | 8 | 5 |
| Complexity | High | 6 | 12 | 4 |
| | Low | 5 | 13 | 4 |
| Criticality | High | 7 | 10 | 2 |
| | Low | 6 | 10 | 3 |
| Governance Responsibility | Internal | 4 | 12 | 5 |
| | External | 5 | 13 | 3 |
| Implementation Responsibility | Technical | 4 | 9 | 5 |
| | Business | 5 | 9 | 4 |
| Scope of Impact | Broad | 5 | 12 | 4 |
| | Limited | 5 | 9 | 7 |

From Table 6.6 we can see the decision distributions in the two rows are identical. Thus, factor *aspect of change* is considered to be a non-affecting factor because regardless of the change being simple or complex, experts favored independent modelling. We use the difference in the number of votes across the two values of a factor to distinguish affecting factors from non-affecting factors. If the difference is within or equal to 3, which is the roundup integer of 10% of the number of participants, both for integrated and independent modelling, then the factor is considered to be non-affecting.

We combine the importance and effect of factors in Table 6.7, with factors in each cell ordered by their rankings in Table 6.5. The table shows that 4 out of the 6 top 50% factors are affecting factors, and 5 out of the 6 bottom 50% factors are non-affecting factors. *Criticality* and *awareness of impact* are non-affecting factors, although they are important; while *rule source* is an affecting factor although ranked lowest in importance.

In the following, we will analyse each affecting factor and derive modelling guidance given the factors' circumstances.

**Table 6.7.** Factor importance and effect matrix

| Importance | Affecting | Non-affecting |
|---|---|---|
| Top 50% | Agility<br>Rate of Change<br>Reusability<br>Accessibility | Criticality<br>Awareness of Impact |
| Bottom 50% | Rule Source | Complexity<br>Governance Responsibility<br>Scope of Impact<br>Aspect of Change<br>Implementation Responsibility |

**Table 6.8.** Dominant modelling preferences

| Factor | Value | Integrate | Separate | Vote difference | Dominant view |
|---|---|---|---|---|---|
| Agility | High | 2 | 15 | 13 | Independent |
|  | Low | 7 | 8 | 1 | Either |
| Rate of Change | Frequent | 1 | 18 | 17 | Independent |
|  | Infrequent | 11 | 6 | −5 | Integrated |
| Reusability | High | 0 | 20 | 20 | Independent |
|  | Low | 10 | 7 | −3 | Integrated |
| Accessibility | High | 5 | 13 | 8 | Independent |
|  | Low | 7 | 8 | 1 | Either |
| Rule Source | Internal | 5 | 6 | 1 | Either |
|  | External | 1 | 11 | 10 | Independent |

Table 6.8 lists the decisions regarding the specific value for each factor. A modelling decision can be derived if the difference in votes is at least 3, which is the roundup integer of 10% of the number of participants; otherwise the votes can be interpreted as not providing a dominant view of the appropriate type of modelling (noted in Table 6.8 as "Either"). For example, for factor *agility*, when the need for agility is high, there are 13 more experts voting for independent modelling than for integrated modelling, so independent modelling is the dominant view for rule modelling. We note that there are three situations in which the experts could not agree on a modelling decision. We have derived six modelling guidelines from the situations that have dominant decisions:

When a business rule has relatively high agility, it should be modelled independently.

When a business rule changes frequently, it should be modelled independently.

When a business rule changes infrequently it should be integrated with a business process model.

When a business rule is highly reusable, it should be modelled independently.

When a business rule's reusability is low, it should be integrated with a business process model.
When a business rule requires relatively high accessibility, it should be modelled independently.

To provide further insights into the rationale of the responses, in the following we highlight relevant insights for non-affecting factors, which were collected through an open-ended comment section in our survey. We use symbol $P$ followed by a number as the participant id.

**Criticality.** The opinions on rule criticality are conflicting. Participants argue that "it's obviously more important that critical business rules are modelled in safe and reliable ways than for less critical roles" (*P20*) and "criticality is important for the enforcement or monitoring of rule violations" (*P11*), but "that doesn't tell us anything about whether the rule can be embedded in the business process or not" (*P20*), and "whether this is done through a BRMS or a BPMS or manually does not matter, as long as it is effective." (*P11*)

**Awareness of Impact.** Awareness of impact "could not always be estimated and could not be easily represented" (*P10*), and "a rule may impact a process or something else" (*P11*), thus it is considered as a less important factor.

**Complexity.** Since "*BPMN is not suitable for BR modelling*" (*P17*), both simple and complex business rules can be easier to handle in a dedicated rule representation than being integrated with a business process model.

**Governance Responsibility.** The importance of governance responsibility is challenged, as "a business rule can be modelled separately and be embedded in a business process at the same time" *(P20)*, and "it depends on if the process model [is] executed by a BPMS or [if] a rulebook be used". *(P16)*

**Scope of Impact.** Participants admit that "it might be easier to see which swim lanes are affected by the rule change and how a separately modelled and maintained BR scope is hard to understand from a single BR out of context" *(P17)*. However, they believe that the factor scope of impact "has more to do with governance and documentation than with modelling" *(P17)*.

**Aspect of Change.** "If the rule logic changes, it's easier to handle in the dedicated rule representation. If a single parameter changes, it's still easier to handle in a dedicated rule representation" *(P11)*. So, the preference is always modelling rules independently, regardless of whether the rule change is complex or simple.

**Implementation Responsibility.** Participants point out that "*business and technical users have different responsibilities for the same set of rules*" (*P12*), with the underlying assumption that the modelling of processes and the implementation processes are separated in practice.

## 6.6   Chapter Summary

In this chapter, we presented the methodology for factor identification, evaluation and decision analysis. Then we presented the identified factors and the evaluation of the factors. Finally, we presented the six guidelines based on the data analysis from the factor evaluation.

# Chapter 7
# A Business Rule Modelling Decision Framework

## 7.1 Overview

In this chapter, we present the development and outcome of the rule modelling decision framework. The objective of the decision framework is to guide modellers on whether to integrate a business rule with a business process model and how to integrate towards achieving the benefits of integrated modelling. As this study related to the design of an artefact, the research methodology of this study is Design Science. Design Science is the research method used to create artefacts aimed to solve identified problems in practice [86]. The artefacts of design science can be constructs, models, methods, or instantiations [87]. In this study, the artefact is the decision framework that will help business rule modellers decide whether to model a business rule within a business process model.

Successful design science research needs to follow a commonly accepted design science methodology rather than to justify the research paradigm on an ad hoc basis with each new paper. Peffers et al. [86] proposed and developed a design science research methodology for the production and presentation of design science research in IS. The design science research process proposed in [86] includes six activities, viz. problem identification and motivation, objectives definition, design and development, demonstration, evaluation, and communication. Problem identification and motivation is intended to define the specific research problem and justify the value of a solution. Objectives definition is needed to infer the objectives of a solution from the problem definition and knowledge of what is possible and feasible. Design and development relates to creating the artifact, including determining the artefact's desired functionality and its architecture and then creating the actual artifact. Resources required for moving from objectives to design and development include knowledge that can be brought to bear in a solution. Demonstration is needed in order to demonstrate the use of the artifact to solve one or more instances of the problem using experimentation, simulation, case study, proof, or other appropriate methods. Evaluation relates to observations and other

© Springer Nature Switzerland AG 2019

W. Wang, *Integrating Business Process Models and Rules*, LNBIP 343,

https://doi.org/10.1007/978-3-030-11809-9_7

investigative means to evaluate how well the artifact supports a solution to the problem. Finally, communication is intended to communicate the problem and the artifact to researchers and other relevant audiences such as practicing professionals when appropriate.

We introduce this study following the design science methodology proposed in [86]. First, we introduce the problem identification and definition of objectives. Then we introduce the design of the decision framework, followed by the demonstration. Given the time and tool development demands to evaluate the decision framework, the evaluation was deemed outside the scope of this thesis. Thus, we only introduce an outline of how such a study can be carried out.

## 7.2  Problem Identification and Definition of Objectives

Due to complex and fragmented enterprise systems and modelling landscapes, organizations struggle to cope with change propagation, compliance management and interoperability. Two aspects related to the above are business process models and business rules, both of which have a role to play in the enterprise setting. Redundancy and inconsistency between business rules and business process models is prevalent, highlighting the need for consideration of integrated modelling of the two. An important prerequisite of achieving integrated modelling is the ability to decide whether a rule should be integrated with a business process model or modelled independently, since integration with graphical business process models [8] may not be suitable is all situations. It follows then that an important aspect of integrated modelling is the understanding of such situations and how they influence business rule representation. While the decision in regards to how a rule should be modelled is not a straightforward one, little guidance exists that can help modellers make such a decision. The wrong decision will increase the cost of system mainte-nance, reduce business process flexibility, and jeopardize compliance. For example, if a business rule that governs a task that exists in several business process models is integrated with all relevant models, multiple instances of that rule need to be updated if it changes, increasing the risk of inconsistency as well as the amount of re-work involved. On the contrary, modelling such a business rule independently in a rule repository, and linking it to relevant models, will make the rule easier to manage since there is only one business rule instance. Another example is when a business rule specifying the roles that can execute a certain activity in a process is represented separately from the process model. In such a case it is possible that a process executor only follows the process model and ignores the rule, which can lead to missed or unauthorized activities and potentially a compliance breech. Thus, the objective of this study is to develop a decision framework that guides modellers on whether to integrate a business rule with a business process model.

## 7.3 The Design and Development of the Decision Framework

**Requirement Analysis of the Decision Framework**

Our decision framework is a type of a decision support system. A decision support system consists of 3 basic components. The inputs, the outputs, and the model. The inputs are numbers and characteristics to analyse in the model. Some inputs cannot be directly obtained and need to be analysed using user knowledge and expertise. The outputs are decision results generated by the decision support system based on user inputs and the calculation of the model. The model part analyses data from the input and generates the decision result as the output. The form of model varies given different decision making problems.

The inputs include a process model repository, a rule repository, and the modeller's inputs of the characteristics of a rule such as the need of accessibility, agility, change frequency, the need of reusability, etc. The modeller's knowledge about the rule, the relevant process models, the modelling languages and systems being used, and other organizational settings are essential for the modeller to measure the characteristics of a rule. For example, how many process models are constrained by a rule will determine the need of reusability, different modelling languages will determine if a rule can be diagrammatically embedded in a process model, and the cost of rule integration are different using different systems and tools. Decision makers, i.e. the modellers, are given a set of business rules, and a set of process models which are constrained by the set of rules. Then, the modeller should study each rule, and the process models that are constrained by this rule, to make the decision that for each process model, should this business rule be integrated or not. Besides the understanding of the rules and models, the modeller should also have a comprehensive knowledge of the organizational setting, including what languages are used for process modelling and rule modelling, what systems manage the rules and the process models, how extensively business rules are used in the organization, etc.

The outputs of the decision framework are the four possible solutions of how to model a business rule, including (1) modelling the rule separately, (2) linking the rule with related process models, (3) diagrammatically embedding the rule, or (4) embedding the rule as texts.

The outputs are means to reach the objectives of the decision framework, which include (1) to improve the understanding of processes and rules to support process-aware system design, audit, process compliance management, staff training, and knowledge management and other functions, (2) to reduce the update cost of frequently changing rules, (3) to support quick changes of rules that require high agility, (4) to improve the reusability of rules that apply in various processes, and (5) to improve the accessibility of rules. The model part of the decision framework takes the inputs, and indicates the output that can improve the understanding of processes and rules, to save the change cost of frequently changed rules, support the quick change of agility rules, improve the reusability of reusable rules, and improve the accessibility of rules which needs high accessibility. Thus, our decision framework incorporates multiple criteria in the model component, and falls in the category of multi-criteria decision-making (MCDM) problems [171].

MCDM involve multiple conflicting criteria in decision making. In multi-criteria decision-making problems, there is no decision that can satisfy all criteria since one criterion conflicts with the others. Any decision has to sacrifice at least one criterion and the decision maker has to find the appropriate decision, which can minimize the loss by incorporating preference information. A widely used way is to assign different weights to each criterion and score each decision only considering each criterion individually. The final score of each decision is the weighted sum up of the scores for each criterion and the appropriate decision is the one which has the highest score. This is the so called analytic hierarchy process (AHP) method [172]. AHP provides a rational framework for structuring a decision problem. AHP decomposes a decision problem into several sub problems and analyses each sub problem independently. A decision maker systematically evaluates the candidate decisions by comparing them to each other two at a time, using the decision maker's own judgments about the decision's relative meaning and importance. Other typical methods include TOPSIS [173], influence diagram [174], SMAA, to name a few [175].

Due to the requirements of our decision framework, current methods to solve MCDM problems are not suitable for our decision framework. First, all MCDM problem-solving methods are aimed to solve a single or limited decision problems. For example, to select a chair from a set of candidates, or select a project for a company. In our case, we are not just selecting one appropriate modelling solution for a business rule. Instead, we use the decision framework to select an appropriate modelling solution for every rule in the organization.

Second, although each MCDM problem-solving method uses different calculation method to calculate the final result, all MCDM problem-solving methods need to assign weights to each criterion, and assign scores to each candidate solution considering each criterion. In other words, these MCDM problem-solving methods highly rely on the quantitative data inputs. However, in our framework, the score of each candidate solution cannot be assigned without considering the characteristics of each business rule, and the appropriate solution for a business rule could be different given different organizational settings, such as modelling languages used in the organization. Thus it is not possible to assign fixed scores to the candidate solutions considering each criterion, or assign fixed weights to each criterion. Instead of simple numbers, the nature of this decision problem relies heavily on a modeller's analysis of the characteristics of each specific business rules, the related process models, the characteristics of the languages and system used in the organization.

Third, MCDM problem-solving methods like AHP consider all criteria at the same level and differentiate them with different weights, rather than priority, and make the final decision in a single step, which weakens the explanation power of the decision system. As our decision framework is different from commonly used MCDM problem-solving methods, which are widely accepted, explainability is essential in our context. The framework is unlikely to be widely adopted in practice unless the decisions suggested by the decision framework are well explained and the modellers understand the reasoning for the suggested modelling approach. Thus, our decision framework cannot construct all the criteria at the same level, and calculate them all at once in a black box to generate a final result. To the contrary, our decision framework needs to make the decision step by step, and ensure that at each step the modeller can see why a decision path is appropriate until the modeller reaches the final solution.

To summarize, our decision framework aims to support decision making for a set of rules using qualitative data based on the decision maker's analysis of the characteristics of each specific business rules, the related process models, the characteristics of the languages and system used in the organization, in a step by step manner that the decision maker can see why a decision path is appropriate at each step until a final solution is reached.

**Constructing the Decision Model**
As introduced in [87], an essential part of design science is the underlying knowledge that informs the design and development of the artefact. The design of the decision framework follows a search process, proposed by [87]. Hevner [87] suggested to design artefacts as a search process where the design will be achieved through searching solutions to sub-problems that constitute the main problem. Then heuristic problem-solving strategies are used to design solutions to each sub-problem so that the design of the final artefact will be built systematically. In the design activity, knowledge of theory that can be brought to bear in a solution is an essential resource required for moving from objectives to the design and development of the artefact [86]. In the following, first we introduce the knowledge building activities we carried out to answer the questions that underpin the model of the decision framework and the knowledge we developed, then we explain how we use the knowledge we to construct the decision model.

**Knowledge Building**
The knowledge underpinning the decision to integrate a business rule within a business process model can span several aspects. This includes knowledge required to answer the basic questions that may arise when undertaking such a decision. We argue that this knowledge is largely missing from current literature. The questions that outline the essential aspects of the decision making process, relate to whether (and when) rule integration should be considered (Q1); what are the factors that affect rule integration and how to reason with them (Q2–Q4) and, if rule integration becomes necessary, which integration method is most suitable. (Q5–Q6):

Q1: Whether rule integration can improve process model understanding?
Q2: What are the factors affecting rule integration?
Q3: How important is each factor?
Q4: How does each factor affect rule integration?
Q5: What are the integration methods?
Q6: Which integration method to use, i.e. how to integrate?

The first question is the basic motivation for rule integration. If the answer is no, there is no motivation for rule integration thus a decision framework is not required. The second and third questions aim to discover the core components in the decision framework. The fourth question provides knowledge for the design of the decision paths at each decision point. The fifth and sixth questions provide knowledge for the integration method to choose. As knowledge to answer these questions is absent from current body of knowledge, we have to generate the requisite knowledge in order to solve these sub-problems.

In the following, we introduce five knowledge building activities we carried out and the knowledge we generated and evaluated to ensure that the design of the decision framework is adequately informed.

1. Theoretical Analysis of Rule Integration and Process Model Understanding

This knowledge building activity tries to answer the question of how rule integration can improve understanding from a theoretical perspective and to motivate the evaluation. As presented in Chap. 4, the decision framework can only be meaningful when rule integration can improve process model understanding. The purpose of theoretical analysis is to find theoretical support from cognitive load and information representation theories that integrating (including all forms of integrating, namely linking, text embedding, and diagrammatically embedding) a business rule within a process model can improve human understanding. The improvement of understanding is the core and fundamental purpose of rule integration, which is a prerequisite of other benefits we can get from rule integration, such as better communication, and better governance, risk management and control. The analysis provides theoretical underpinnings that motivate the empirical evaluation that can answer the first question, which is whether integrating business rules with business process models can improve the understanding of business process models.

2. Empirical Evaluation of Rule Integration and Process Model Understanding

This knowledge building activity tries to empirically evaluate *whether* rule integration can improve process model understanding. We argue that the evaluation step in design science can also target each component of the artefact since a high quality artefact can be developed when each of its components is proven to be reliable. Thus, theoretical analysis alone is not sufficient, the argument that rule integration can improve process model understanding needs to be authentically evaluated and tested. As presented in Chap. 3, experimental evaluation is the most suitable research method to test such an argument. As introduced in Chap. 5, we carried out an experiment, investigating the effect of process model understanding of a specific rule integration approach, rule linking, which uses graphical links to connect process model symbols with rules. Our experiment findings indicate that linked rules can improve the understanding of business processes and rules, which answered our first sub-problem which is whether rule integration can improve process model understanding.

3.  Rule Integration Factors Identification

Given a confirmed answer of the *whether* question, we can start to build knowledge of the sub-question of *what*, that is what are the factors that affect the decision of integrating business rules with business process models. The factors are the essential components in the decision framework. As introduced in Chap. 6, the knowledge building of this question of *what* was accomplished through a literature review of important Computer Science and Information Science articles in the past 20 years. The factor identification followed a keyword selection, manual filtering, coding and analysis procedure. Then the candidate factors found in each article were coded and refined and finally twelve factors were identified.

4.  Rule integration Factors Evaluation

The factors were evaluated after they were identified. The evaluation built knowledge of (1) how important is each factor and (2) how does each factor affect rule integration decision. As presented in Chap. 7, the evaluation was done via an online survey. Surveys can be used as a research tool to collect knowledge and opinion from experts and thus is an accepted approach to empirically validate factors [176]. The survey involved experts who were authors of the papers in which the factors were identified through our literature review. The indication of the importance of each factor and the modelling decisions given by experts were used to decide which factor should be included in the decision framework, and factors that experts could not agree on were discarded. The knowledge collected to answer the question of how does each factor affect the decision of rule integration is used to answer the question of "when" to use rule integration.

5.  Business Rule Modelling Approaches Classification

The business rule modelling approach classification provides knowledge to answer the question of "which" rule integration method to use to integrate business rules. A prerequisite of answering the question of "which" rule integration method to use is to find out what are the possible options that a process modeller can choose from. Chapter 2 introduces an analysis of rule integration approaches, and classifies them into three categories, viz. linking, text embedding, and diagrammatical embedding. The three categories of rule integration approaches are the options for the question of "which". Combined with the knowledge of the *how* each factor affects the decision of rule integration, we cannot only focus the question of *when* to use rule integration but also answer the question of *when* to use *which* integration method.

**Constructing the Decision Framework Using Knowledge**

As introduced in the knowledge building section of this chapter, we built three pieces of knowledge for this decision framework: First, we found through our empirical study that rule integration can indeed improve the understanding of business process models. Second, we identified factors that influence the decision of rule integration, and how these factors affect such a decision. Third, we identified three rule integration methods. We construct the decision model of our decision framework using the knowledge in the following.

**Integrating the Knowledge of Integration and Process Model Understanding**
The fundamental benefit of rule integration is to help modellers, system designers, process participants and other stakeholders to understand a business process model better, thus to achieve better communication, better system design, better compliance management and so on. Our decision framework makes the decision step by step, to ensure that with each step the modeller can understand why a decision path is suggested, until the modeller reaches the final solution. Thus, the improvement of business process model understanding becomes one of the criteria in the first decision point.

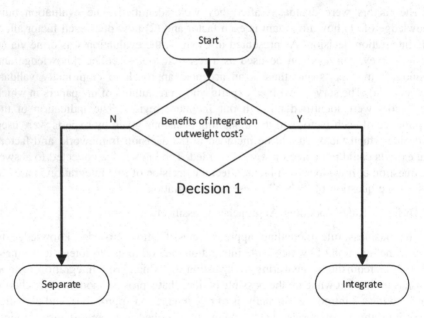

**Fig. 7.1.** The first decision point illustration

The first issue a modeller should consider is whether there is a significant need to improve process model understanding. The modeller should have the knowledge of whether current and future process model users understand the process model well in terms of the constraints or requirements that are specified in the rule. Do variations of work happen in the execution of the process model due to the process participant's incorrect understanding of the constraints and requirements that are specified in rules? Is it difficult for new process model users of a different background to easily and fully understand the constraints specified in the rule? If the answer is yes, then there is a need to integrate the rule in the process model. However, achieving better understanding will incur integration costs. Time and human resources are required to integrate a rule with a process model in an appropriate way. Thus, whether the benefits of integration of a rule can outweigh the cost is the first question that needs to be considered in the process of decision making. If the resources needed to implement the integration exceed the benefits, then the appropriate decision should be leave the rule separate as it is. Otherwise, if the integration of a rule can largely improve the understanding of a process model and avoid the misunderstanding in the design of information systems or in the execution of the process model, and thus improvement can overcome the cost of integration, then the appropriate decision should be to integrate the rule. The first decision point of the decision framework is illustrated in Fig. 7.1.

**Integrating the Knowledge of Rule Integration Methods**
If the decision from the earlier decision point is to integrate, then the next step is to decide which of the three integration methods are appropriate.

We design the decision logic of the second decision step based on the differences of the three integration methods, and knowledge of the factors we identified and evaluated, which are introduced in Chap. 6. In the following, we first restate the differences of the link method with the embedding methods. Then, we restate the differences of the two embedding methods, i.e. text embedding and diagrammatic embedding.

As introduced in Sect. 2.6, there are three business rule integration methods. One method is link, and the other two methods are text embedding and diagrammatical embedding. The link method is differentiated from embedding methods in several ways.

Using the link method, business rules are not part of a process model, but only connected with a process model. The process model and the rules are managed by different systems. Thus, a linked rule can be accessed separately without the need to access a process model, and can be reused without the need to detach it from the process model and to replicate it. Linked rules are more flexible than embedded rules in two ways. First, linked rules are executed directly by the rule engine and hence they can be added or removed when needed. Second, when the rule is changed, all links that refer to same rule from different process models will be automatically up to date - changing a linked rule requires less time.

Using text embedding, a business rule is represented in the form of text in a graphical business process model. For example, BPMN has a text annotation construct that allows users to specify business rules into such an annotation construct in sentential format. Using diagrammatic embedding, a business rule is represented in the form of graphical symbols, such as sequence flows, gateways and other symbols in a business process model. The two embedding methods model business rules inside a process model, and the business rules are regarded as a part of a process model. Business rules are managed together with a process model by the same system. For example, a BPMN editor can be used to edit the process models as well as the rules represented in text annotations or diagrammatical symbols. Thus, accessing an embedded rule needs to access to the process model, and an embedded rule first needs to be replicated thus to be reused in other process models. Using embedding methods, any addition or removal of activities requires changes in the existing process and hence the underlying implementation, and a change to a rule will not automatically update the same rule embedded in other processes. Thus more time and effort are needed to update the rules and manage their consistency.

On the other hand, embedding methods can outweigh the link method by reducing the cognitive cost of information interpretation and comprehension. Information presented in an integrated manner is considered to reduce cognitive load, while split-source information can generate a heavy cognitive load in the process of information assimilation [97]. Accordingly, in the context of process and rule modelling, embedding business rules into relevant business process models can reduce cognitive load and improve the understanding of business processes. Although the link method can help users to navigate to the content of the linked rules, the process model and the rules are still in different sources. The processing of such linked, but mutually referring information, frequently and unnecessarily requires attention to be split and switched between different sources which inevitably consumes part of available working memory capacity and decreases cognitive resources available for learning [98, 99]. Thus, embedding methods can outweigh the link method in terms of better cognitive efficiency.

**Integrating the Knowledge of Factors Affecting the Decision**
We design the decision logic of the second decision step based on the differences of the three integration methods, and knowledge of the factors we identified and evaluated. In the following, we will introduce how we select the factors as criteria for the second decision point to decide the appropriate integration method.

As introduced in Chap. 1, we identified twelve factors that can affect the rule integration decision, and we evaluated the factors via a survey with experts. The evaluation of the factors is based on two dimensions. The first dimension is the importance of each factor, and the second dimension is if a factor has a clear effect on the decision to integration a rule. To properly incorporate the factors into the decision framework, we need to discard the factors which are not important and the factors which are not affecting the decision, and only consider the factors that are both important and affecting the rule integration decision. Four of the twelve factors meet these criteria, which are agility, rate of change, reusability, and accessibility. Agility refers to how quickly a business rule needs to be adapted due to a change. Rate of Change refers to the frequency with which a business rule requires modification. Reusability refers to the need for a rule to be used in other process models to reduce the resources required in developing new rules. Accessibility refers to the business user's need to view a business rule in a format that is suitable to his or her need. We asked experts for the their opinion on how a rule should be modelled given different situations of each factor, and the dominant views are shown in Table 6.8. To summarize, when the need of agility, the rate of change, the need of accessibility, and the need of reuse of a business rule is high, the indication from experts is to model the business rule in an independent manner, rather than embed the business rule inside a business process model. The decision aligns well with the differences between the link method and the two embedding methods.

The two embedding methods model business rules inside a process model, and the business rules are regarded as a part of a process model. Business rules are managed together with a process model by the same system.

In terms of the need of agility and rate of change, any modification, including addition and removal of embedded business rules requires changes in the existing process, which take more time and thus affect agility. Agility is about how much time each change takes, and rate of change is about how often a rule needs to be changed. A frequently changing embedded rule will cost more time and effort to manage than a relatively stable embedded rule. On the other hand, linked rules are more flexible than embedded rules as linked rules are executed directly by the rule engine and hence they can be added or removed when needed.

In terms of the need of reuse, an embedded rule is part of a process model. It first needs to be separated from the process model thus to be reused in other process models. Every process model that is constrained by the rule owns a copy of the rule. If the rule requires an update, then every copy of the rule needs to be updated. On the other hand, all process models that are constrained by the rule refer to the same copy of the rule. Thus when the rule is changed, all references of the rule are updated automatically.

In terms of the need of accessibility, when requiring access to an embedded rule one needs to access the process model and locate, read or update the rule. On the other hand, a linked rule can be accessed in the rule management system separately without the need to access a process model.

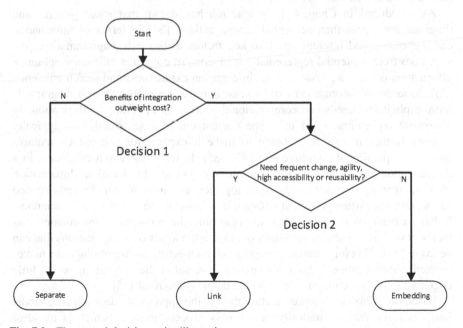

**Fig. 7.2.**  The second decision point illustration

As the embedding methods can have better cognitive efficiency than the link method, but the link method can solve the problems in terms of agility, high rate of change, reusability, and accessibility, for the second decision point, the overall decision logic is: For a given business rule, if the need for any of the high agility, frequent change, high accessibility, or high reusability is essential, the appropriate rule integration method is link. Otherwise, the appropriate rule integration method is embedding. For example, let us consider a business rule that only constrains a single process model, doesn't need high accessibility or agility, and does not need change in the future. In this case, the appropriate decision is to embed the rule. If we change one condition, that the rule requires frequent changes, and keep the other three conditions the same, then, in this case, the decision is to link the rule to save time and resources needed to make frequent changes. If we further change another condition - that the rule constrains activities in several process models - and keep the other two conditions the same, then, in this case, the decision is still to link the rule. Since if we embed the business rule in every process model, then when the rule requires change, every copy of the rule needs to be changed. The second decision point of the decision framework is illustrated in Fig. 7.2.

### Integrating the Knowledge of Diagrammatic Representation

The third step is to make a decision with respect to text embedding and diagrammatic embedding. We design this decision based on the differences between diagrammatic representation and sentential representation that we introduced in Chap. 4, because not all business rules can be diagrammatically represented in business process models [5, 6, 8].

As introduced in Chap. 4, prior research has shown that static pictures and diagrams are better than sentential representations [34] in terms of information comprehension and inferencing. Two key factors distinguish diagrammatic representations from sentential representations in terms of cognition efficiency in human information processing systems - viz. information explicitness and search efficiency [35]. In terms of information explicitness, information represented in diagrams is more explicit and needs less computational effort [34]. In contrast, informationally equivalent representation of the same content but in a sentential form typically requires further mental formulation to make it explicit for use, which requires greater computational cognitive effort [34, 35]. In terms of search efficiency, in a diagrammatic representation information is organized by location. Information elements that are relevant are grouped together, and information elements needed for inference are often present at adjacent locations, or connected with associations. Relations between graphical elements map onto the relations of information elements in such a way that they restrict or enforce the kinds of interpretations that can be made [34]. This information grouping and connecting nature of diagrams makes problem solving proceed through a smooth traversal of the diagram, in which little cognitive effort in terms of search computation is required [35].

Based on information representation theory, the appropriate decision is to model business rules diagrammatically in business process models, which is an ideal solution. However, it is well studied in current literature that not all business rules

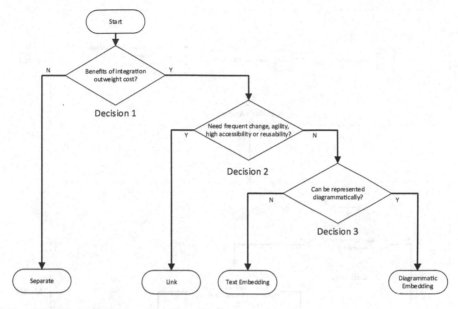

**Fig. 7.3.** The third decision point illustration

can be diagrammatically represented in business process models due to the representational capacities of current business process modelling languages [5, 6, 8]. Thus, the decision for the third step is: if a business rule can be diagrammatically represented in a process model, the decision of rule integration is to use diagrammatical embedding. Otherwise, the decision of rule integration is to use text embedding. In practice, whether a business rule can be diagrammatically represented depends on the content of the rule, and the process modelling language that is used in the organization. The third decision point of the decision framework is illustrated in Fig. 7.3.

### The Decision Framework

The final decision framework is illustrated in Fig. 7.4. We choose to represent the decision framework as a flow chart, as it provides a visual and succinct way of expressing our step-by-step decision making model.

As illustrated in Fig. 7.4, the decision framework consists of three parts, i.e. the input, the model, and the output.

The input component of the framework refers to the set of business rules that need to be considered, and the business process models that are constrained by the business rules. It also encompasses the organizational setting, such as the process and rule management systems, tools, and modelling languages used in the organization. These inputs need to be considered by the decision maker, i.e. the modeller, before applying the decision model.

The model component of the framework consists of three decision points. Given a set of business rules, decision point 1 makes a decision between separation and

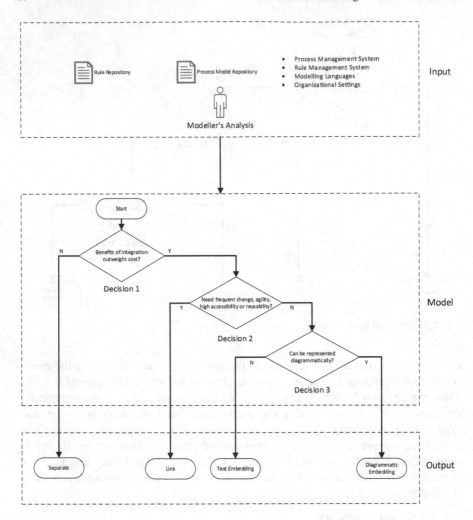

**Fig. 7.4.** The decision framework

integration. The decision logic of decision point 1 is: Whether the benefits of integration of a rule can outweigh the cost. If the resources needed to implement the integration exceed the benefits, then the decision should be leave the rule separate as it is. Otherwise, if the integration of a rule can improve the understanding of a process model and avoid the misunderstanding in the execution of the process model, i.e. improvement outweighs the cost of integration, then the decision should be to integrate the rule.

Decision point 2 makes a decision between link and embedding. The decision logic of decision point 2 is: For a given business rule, if the need for any of the high agility, frequent change, high accessibility, or high reusability is essential, the appropriate rule integration method is link. Otherwise, the appropriate rule integration method is embedding.

   Decision point 3 makes a decision between text embedding and diagrammatical embedding. The decision logic for decision point 3 is: If a business rule can be diagrammatically represented in a process model, the appropriate decision of rule integration is to use diagrammatical embedding. Otherwise, the appropriate decision of rule integration is to use text embedding.

   The output part consist of four candidate decisions, i.e. separation, link, text embedding, and diagrammatical embedding. Separation is selected as the decision if a business rule is already well understood and enhanced in business process executions, or the cost of the rule integration outweighs the benefits from improved understanding. Link is selected as the decision when the decision in the previous decision point is integration, and the rule changes frequently, requires high agility, reusability or accessibility. Text embedding is selected as the decision when the decision in the previous decision point is embedding, but the rule cannot be represented diagrammatically due to the content of the rule and the representation limitations of the modelling language used in the organization. Diagrammatical embedding is selected as the decision when the decision in the previous decision point is embedding, and the rule can be properly represented in a diagrammatical manner using the modelling language that is used in the organization.

## 7.4   The Decision Framework Demonstration

The Demonstration step in the design science methodology proposed by [86] is used to demonstrate the use of the artefact to solve one or more instances of the problem using experimentation, simulation, case study, or other appropriate activity [86]. We demonstrate how the decision framework can be used by adopting the simulated car repair process model that we used in our experiment as introduced in Chap. 5. The process model shown in Fig. 7.5 represents a car repair process of a car service company.

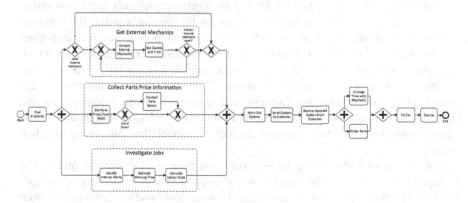

**Fig. 7.5.** Car repair process model before rule integration

We use 4 business rules that constrain this process to demonstrate how the decision framework is used in practice. The 4 business rules are:

Rule 1: If there is any problem that can only be fixed by external mechanics in activity 'Find Problems', then activity group 'Get External Mechanics' must be executed.

Rule 2: If a customer has spent over 2,000 in the past 12 months, then the customer can have a 10% discount on the internal labour cost, a 5% discount on the external labour cost, and a 2% discount on the parts.

Rule 3: Only the works that will be done by internal mechanics need to be identified in activity 'Identify Internal Works'.

Rule 4: Both prices for a brand-new part and a second-hand part must be collected in activity group 'Collect Parts Price Information'.

Before investigating each rule, the manager, who is the decision maker, investigates the modelling tools used in this car repair company. The process modelling language used in the company is BPMN which supports text annotations. The rules are simply modelled using natural language. The company uses a process aware information system that can guide the staff to perform each activity in the process model following the control flow. The business rules are managed by a tool that supports navigating to each rule via URLs. Thus, the manager finds that the cost of rule integration is small given the systems and tools used in the company. Then for each of the 4 rules, the manager decides how to integrate it following the decision framework.

Rule 1 is about contacting external mechanics to do repair jobs that cannot be handled by internal mechanics. The manager has found that this rule has been understood and followed well in the past and no operation that is against this rule happened in the past, and new users can easily understand and remember this rule after adequate training. Thus, following our decision framework, in the first decision point, the manager decides to leave the rule in a separate format as it was.

Rule 2 is about the discount policy, which specifies the allowed discounts for different part of the total quote. The manager has found that the discount policy is not well executed in the past, which led to several complaints from customers. Thus, following our decision framework, in the first decision point, the manager decides to integrate this business rule. The discount policy has two important objectives. First is to offer an attractive quote to the customer's comparing with the company's competitors. Second is to boost the sales before the finial year audition, the New Year and other important dates. Thus, the discount percentages are changing frequently against the discount policies of the company's competitors, and changing in different times of a year. Following our decision framework, in the second decision point, the manager decides to model this rule using the link method.

Rule 3 is about identifying labour work and thus to calculate the quote. The manager has found that the breakdown of costs given to customers sometimes includes external labour cost in the internal labour costs section, leading to a poor service quality. Thus, following our decision framework, in the first decision point, the manager decides to integrate this business rule. The manager finds that this rule is used only in this process model, and the rule hasn't been changed for the last year. The manager believes that this rule will remains stable and don't need any agile change in the future. Thus, following our decision framework, in the second decision point, the manager decides to integrate this rule using embedding. After checking the representation capacity of BPMN, which is the process modelling language used in the company, the manager find that it is difficult to represent this rule diagrammatically in the process model, as representing this rule diagrammatically needs several gateways and activities to represent, and needs to change other activities and the control flow in activity group 'Investigate Jobs'. Thus, following our decision framework, in the third decision point, the manager decides to model the business rule using text embedding.

Rule 4 is about collecting data to make the quotes. As customers can have the right to choose using second hand parts and brand new parts, different quotes should be given to them. The manager has found that some customers were only offered the quote for the brand new parts, which leaded to the refusal of the car repair service because of the high cost. Thus, following our decision framework, in the first decision point, the manager decides to integrate this business rule. The manager finds that this rule is used only in this process model, and the rule wasn't changed in the last year. The manager believes that this rule will remain stable for the foreseeable future. Thus, following our decision framework, in the second decision point, the manager decides to integrate this rule using embedding. After checking the representation capacity of BPMN, which is the process modelling language used in the company, the manager find that this rule can be represented properly using a few BPMN symbols. Thus, following our decision framework, in the third decision point, the manager decides to model the business rule using diagrammatic embedding.

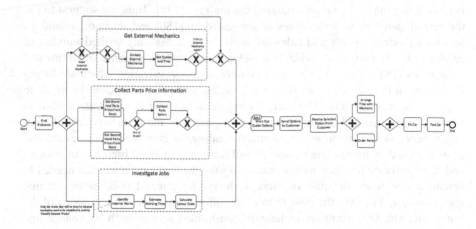

**Fig. 7.6.** The car repair process model after rule integration

Figure 7.6 shows the car repair process model after rule integration. As seen in Fig. 7.6, Rule 1 is not integrated with the process model, Rule 2 is linked to the process model using a linking icon attached to activity 'Work Out Quote Options', Rule 3 is integrated with the process model, using a text annotation attaching to activity 'Identify Internal Works', and Rule 4 is integrated with the process model using activity symbols 'Get Brand-new Parts Prices from Stock and 'Get Second-hand Parts Prices from Stock', and a parallel gateway.

## 7.5   The Decision Framework Evaluation

The evaluation of the framework can be undertaken through a series of empirical and longitudinal investigations in organizational contexts. Such an in-situ study will further require requisite tool support and integration with the business rule software and systems specific to the organization. Given the time and tool development demands of the study, the evaluation was deemed outside the scope of this thesis. Thus, here we only introduce a recommendation of how such a study can be carried out.

The focus of the evaluation is to have a deeper understanding of what consequences the adoption and use of the decision framework has in organizations, and if the decision framework can guide organizations to improve the management of process models and rules. We propose the use of case study research methodology for this study. Case studies observe a subject in real life settings through a period of time, and includes the complex interaction between the researcher and the many parts of the research environment. Case study is a methodology adopted by researchers to study the effect of an artefact or a project in real settings such as in [177, 178]. Thus, case studies match the evaluation requirements of the decision framework.

A selection of an appropriate population can control extraneous variation and help to define the limits for generalizing the findings [179]. Thus, we suggest to use theoretical sampling to select cases as suggested by [180] and select organizations in which process models and rules are actively used. As only limited number of cases can be studied, it is advisable to select cases such as extreme situations and polar types [181]. Thus, we suggest that only select organization which are facing difficulties in the management of process models and rules, and have the needs to improve the management. The includes organizations that demonstrate a need to improve the shared understanding of business processes and rules between different departments, or at least to avoid misunderstanding, to improve process executers' awareness and understanding of operational rules thus to avoid breaches of policies and to improve compliance management, to save the time and resources needed to update a rule when the rule requires a change by internal policies or external regulations, and to save the cost to manage different instances and versions of the same rule, etc. Organizations in heavily constrained sectors such as finance and health industry could be ideal candidates for the case study.

As the consequences of adopting the decision framework can be experienced in different ways by different people [178], we suggest to collect data from people of different roles, different management levels and different departments who are involved in the use of process models and rules. The example roles can be process modellers, rule and policy designers, IT development and IT support team, internal auditors, process executors, etc.

A set of rules and process models will be selected as the target for the decision framework. The selection of rules and process models should also fill theoretical categories and provide examples of polar types [179] to support generalizing the findings. Thus, to evaluate the decision framework, the characteristics of rules and process models that should be covered in the selection will include but not be limited to (1) the need for understanding, (2) the change frequency, (3) the need for agility, (4) the need for reusability, and (5) the need for accessibility. Moreover, both of the two polar values of a characteristic should be selected. For example, rules that change frequently and those that remain stable should both be selected, and process models that operate within a department and those that are shared between different departments should both be selected.

To evaluate the decision framework, the framework needs to be implemented as a decision support system which integrates with existing systems in the organization. By integrating the decision support system with other systems in the organization, the decision support system can collect data that can provide essential information to the decision makers from other systems. The information can largely improve the ease of use of the decision systems by saving the decision maker's time and effort in collecting data. For example, The Red Hat JBoss BPM Suite[1] and BRMS[2] are open-sources business process and business rule management systems which can produce essential data which are needed in the decision making. By integrating with the JBoss BPM Suite and BRMS, the decision support system can automatically collect the following data. It can collect rule change frequency information and agility information from rule edit logs. It can collect performance information and non-compliance information from process execution event logs. It can also collect information of how many process models or activities does a given rule constraints and what they are, and represent this information in a consumable form for the decision maker.

Data collection in the case study can be carried out in two stages, i.e. the pre-deployment stage and the post-deployment stage.

Data collection in the pre-deployment stage needs to capture the state of the organization (in terms of rules and process models management) before the decision support system is implemented, thus to establish a baseline to be compared with the state of the organization after the use of the decision support system. The data can be collected from two types of sources. The first is people, the second is the systems. Semi-structured interviews can be used to collect data from people of

---

[1]https://developers.redhat.com/products/bpmsuite/overview/.

[2]https://developers.redhat.com/products/brms/overview/?referrer=jbd.

different roles of different management levels who are involved in the use of process models and rules. The interviews focus on data about the use of the process models and rules, including how business rules are managed and used in the organization, how business rules are integrated with process models, and the problems that different people have faced in the past, such as compliance problems, system implementation problems, training problems, etc. Casual conversations and meeting archives are other means to collect such data. A variety of data about the process models and rules management state before the adoption and use of the decision support system can be collected from different systems, such as customer management systems, process execution and monitoring systems, rule management systems, audit systems, etc. Data such as the number of customer complaints, number of unexpected process operations and non-compliant behaviours are all directly related with the management of process models and rules.

Data collection in the post deployment focuses on the use of the decision framework, and what the decision framework brings to the organization. Data about the use of the decision support system includes answers to the questions of: How is the decision support system being used by the users to make rule modelling decisions? How much training is needed to use the decision support system? How easily it can be used? What are the problems that occurred during the use? Do the decision makers think that the decision support system is making good quality decisions? How useful is the decision support system from the views of managers, modellers, auditors, and process operators?

Data to answer such questions could be collected not long after the decision support system is implemented. On the other hand, data to answer the questions about what consequences the use of the decision system brings to the organization requires a longitudinal study. As the representation of some rules changes after the use of the decision support system, some separated rules are either linked to process models, texted embedded, or diagrammatically embedded in process models. The consequences can only be observed when activities related to the newly represented rules take place. For example, the cost of rule change can only be observed when rules are changed a few times according to the requirements of internal policies, strategies, or external regulations. The benefits of rule linking can be observed after a rule is further used in more than one process models. Data collected in this stage includes: Have the rule modelling decisions suggested by the decision support system improved the management of process models and rules, in terms of understanding of process models and rules, cost of rule change, rule change agility, accessibility, ease of rule reuse, rate of process misbehaviour, etc.

The data collected in the two stages will allow as have a rich and comprehensive understanding of what happens in practice. By interpreting the data collected, we can have deeper understanding of the effects of different rule integration methods to different process models, rules, people, and systems. The decision framework and the decision support system will go into a redesign phase that incorporates the knowledge interpreted from the data about the ease of use of the decision support system, the quality of the decisions made it, and the difficulties to implement different integration methods, etc.

## 7.6   Chapter Summary

In this chapter, we introduced how we design and develop the rule modelling decision framework. The research methodology of this study is Design Science [86]. We first introduced the problem identification and definition of objectives. Then we present the knowledge that underpins the design of the decision framework. Following this, we introduced the design, demonstration, and an outline of the evaluation of the decision framework.

# Chapter 8
# Conclusion

## 8.1 Overview

Both business processes and business rules focus on creating a representation of the organization's policies and practices. They are complementary modelling approaches as they address distinct aspects of organizational practices. The conceptual and pragmatic overlap between business process models and business rules indicates a need to model the two related aspects together. While researchers have argued that integrated modelling of business process models and business rules can improve the understanding of business processes, this proposition has neither been theoretically analysed nor empirically evaluated. Moreover, there are situations in which a business rule is better modelled independently of a business process model, but also situations in which it is more appropriate to integrate the rule with a business process model.

Thus, the aim of this thesis was to develop a decision framework that guides modellers on whether or not to integrate a business rule with a business process model. Towards this aim, we have undertaken three interrelated studies. This chapter summarises the major contributions of the thesis, the limitations, and an overview of the future work.

## 8.2 Summary of Contributions

In study 1, we found that rue linking can improve user understanding of process models.

Study 1 theoretically analysed and empirically evaluated whether business rule integration can improve business process model understanding. As introduced in Chap. 1, current body of knowledge lacks the knowledge that if such integration can improve understanding, why such integration can improve understanding, and

W. Wang, *Integrating Business Process Models and Rules*, LNBIP 343,
https://doi.org/10.1007/978-3-030-11809-9_8

which aspect of understanding can such integration improves (understanding accuracy, understanding time efficiency, and the cost of mental effort in understanding). Only when we can answer these questions, we can have a deep understanding of rule integration, thus develop modelling languages and methods which can further improve the modelling of processes and rules.

This study used an experiment investigating the effect of process model understanding of a specific rule integration approach, rule linking, which uses graphical links to connect process model symbols with rules. We used a cross-group experiment design with student groups, giving two groups the same process models and rules, but different rule representations. In one group, the rules are linked to process models while separated in the other group. We used comprehension questions to test the understanding accuracy and used an eye-tracker to measure the understanding efficiency.

We focused on 3 aspects of understanding: accuracy, time efficiency, and mental effort. Our results suggest that the use of rule links has a positive effect to all the 3 aspects of understanding as compared to process models with associated rules that are separately available. When investigating the effects to the process model, the rules, and questions individually, our results show that the reduction of time and mental effort in reading the rules contributes most to the overall reduction of time and mental effort.

We also found that while rule links can reduce time spent per visit overall, which is mainly caused by the reduction of time spent per visit in reading the rules, it will not increase the overall number of attention switches in the three areas. Instead, rule links can increase visits to the process model while decrease visits to the rules. By investigating attention switches in the three areas in pairs, we found that linked rules can increase the attention switches between the process model and the questions, and between the process model and the rules, while decrease the attention switches between the rules and the questions. The increase of attention switches between the process model and the rules indicates that given linked rules, participants focus more on integrating information from rules and a process model, and answer questions. The decrease of attention switches between the rules and the questions, and the increase of attention switches between the process model and the questions, indicates that given separated rules, participants relied too much in the rules area to answer the questions, instead of using information from process models, thus resulting a lower quality of understanding.

In study 2, we identified and evaluated factors that can affect rule integration decisions.

Study 2 identified and evaluated factors that will influence the decision as to whether or not a business rule should be integrated with a business process model. As introduced in Chap. 1, there are situations under which a business rule is better modelled independently of a business process model, and also situations under which it is more appropriate to integrate the rule with a business process model. It follows then, that an important aspect of integrated modelling is the understanding of such situations and how they influence business rule representation. While the decision in regards to how a rule should be modelled is not a straightforward one, little guidance exists that can help modellers make such a decision. This short-coming results in fragmented and inconsistent business process and rule models.

In Study 2, we carried out a systematic process of identification of factors that are thought to influence the decision about whether or not to model business rules in an integrated manner. To identify these factors, a systematic literature review was conducted based on a comprehensive set of well-regarded Information Systems and Computer Science journals and conferences and twelve factors were identified. An online survey was carried out with the participation of the authors of the papers that were the sources for the factor identification to validate the identified factors, and to evaluate their relative importance and effects on the decision as to whether a business rule should be integrated with a process model.

We identified from literature twelve factors that potentially influence a decision on whether a business rule should be modelled separately or integrated in a process model. We empirically explored the importance of each identified factor with academic participants, and identified agility as the most important factor, followed by criticality, rate of change, and reusability, while accessibility, awareness of impact, complexity, governance responsibility and scope of impact, with aspect of change, implementation responsibility and rule source being the least important factors. We also explored indications of how a business rule should be modelled given a specific context of each factor, and derived seven guidelines for rule modelling. By following these guidelines in deciding whether to model a business rule separately or integrated in a business process model, process modellers can achieve representations of business operations that facilitate better understanding, maintainability, accessibility, and reusability in terms of business rules.

In study 3, we designed a rule integration decision framework that can help modeller to make informed decision on whether and how to integrate a business rule with a business process model.

Study 3 developed a decision framework that guides modellers on whether or not to integrate a business rule with a business process model. In current literature, there is a lack of guidance outlining the circumstances under which business rules should be integrated in a business process model, yet such a decision is not a straight-forward one. There are situations under which it may be more appropriate to integrate a business rule with a business process model, and situations under which a business rule is better modelled separately from a business process model. The wrong decision will increase the cost of system maintenance, reduce business process flexibility and reusability, and jeopardize compliance.

The decision framework is designed based on knowledge in literature and knowledge built in Study 1 and Study 2, and consists of 3 components: the inputs, the outputs, and the model. The inputs include a process model repository, a rule repository, and the modeller's inputs of the characteristics of a rule such as the need of accessibility, agility, change frequency, the need of reusability, etc. The modeller's knowledge about the rule, the relevant process models, the modelling languages and systems being used, and other organizational settings are essential for the modeller to measure the characteristics of a rule. The outputs of the decision framework are the four possible solutions of how to model a business rule, including (1) model the rule separately, (2) link the rule with related process models, (3) diagrammatically embed the rule, or (4) embed the rule as texts.

The model part of the decision framework follows a step by step manner and contains three decision points thus the decision maker can see why a decision path is selected at each step until a final solution is reached. The decision framework model consists of three decision points. For a given business rules, decision point 1 makes a decision between separation and integration. If the resources need to implement the integration exceed the benefits, then the decision should be leave the rule separate as it is. Otherwise, the decision should be to integrate the rule. Decision point 2 makes a decision between link and embedding. For a given business rule, if the need for any of the high agility, frequent change, high accessibility, or high reusability is essential, the rule integration method is link. Otherwise, the rule integration method is embedding. Decision point 3 makes a decision between text embedding and diagrammatical embedding. If a business rule can be diagrammatically represented in a process model, the decision of rule integration is to use diagrammatical embedding. Otherwise, the decision of rule integration is to use text embedding.

## 8.3 Research Limitations and Future Work

This research is not without limitations. The limitations in study 1 relate to validity of the experiment. In terms of internal validity, our use of a between group repeated measure experiment helped eliminate many confounding factors, and statistics show that the two groups are balanced in experiment performance. However, due to the weak validity of subjective measures about business process and rule models familiarity and domain familiarity, we cannot tell if the two groups are balanced in these aspects. Second, the different layout of screen areas could possibly affect the results. Recall that we have three areas on the screen, viz. Process Model Area, Rules Area and Question Area, and the Rules Area is allocated at the right side of the screen. It is possible that the experiment results will be different if we change the location of each area. For example, if the Rules Area is allocated to the centre of the screen, the rules may be easier to be noticed and information needed may be easier to retrieve. Third, time is a factor that can affect cognitive metrics such as understanding quality. In our experiment, time is a dependent factor instead of a factor, and the results show that in each run of the experiment, the group using linked rules spent less time than the group using separated rules. Thus, our conclusions are not based on the equality of time between the two groups, and some conclusions may not be true given two groups have the same time. For example, the group that using separated rules spent more time in each run, while got lower answer correctness, and we may infer that given equal time, the group using separated rules will have even lower answer correctness so the conclusion 1 remains to be true. However, given equal time, the difference of overall number of attention switch between the two groups may be significant, thus conclusion 9 may not be true.

In terms of construct validity, we operationalized each construct in our study in limited ways. We only used objective measures for quality and efficiency of understanding, and only manipulated the representation of business rules in two ways (linked rules and separated rules), and the questions were designed to test the understanding of the effect of business rules on business process models. Following [52], it would have been ideal if we had measured the perceived quality and efficiency of understanding, manipulated the representation of business rules in other ways such as diagrammatical integration, and asked questions only about a process model itself. Thus, our research results are limited to the treatments, measurements and questions that we used.

Finally, in terms of external validity, we used a sample of university students rather than a sample of practitioners. Moreover, we cannot say that the process models, rules, and questions we used faithfully reflect those used in organizations in practice. Organizations may use more complex process models and lager number of rules, and the tasks may be more challenging. Third, the way that rules are separated from process models in practice are different from our study. In our experiment, rules are positioned side by side with a process model. In practice, rules are scattered around in different sources such as policy and procedure documents, training materials, spreadsheets, which are not side by side with a process model [53]. However, we can generalize that separated rules can result in worse under-standing quality, efficiency and mental effort, when more rules are introduced, and when rules are not side by side with a process model but in other documents or applications. Clearly, more field studies are needed on this topic to investigate how the separation of rules from process models affect under-standing in practice.

Study 2 has three limitations. First, this study focuses on the factors which have a relatively high level of influence. Different modelling languages, tools and integrated modelling methods will affect these factors differently and will be a promising topic for future research. Second, we limit our scope of rules to those that can be both modelled independently as well as modelled with a business process. The rules that do not have the capability to be modelled into processes are beyond our discussion since there is no option for an alternative modelling decision. Although semantics and types of rule can be used to distinguish these rules in some cases, modellers still need to judge each rule individually according to its characteristics. Last, our study participants are predominantly academic experts in the field. The views of common practice are also critical to understand and are the next step in our study. Following that step, we plan to develop a decision framework and prototype to guide business rule modelling decisions. We expect that further empirical study will help to extend the decision framework through deeper insights into the decision processes.

The main limitation of study 3 is that the decision framework is not evaluated in practice. Although we have evaluated the essential constructional components of the decision framework such as the effect of rule linking to understanding, the factors that affect the decision of rule integration, the overall decision framework is not evaluated. The evaluation of the decision framework needs to be undertaken through a series of case studies as it requires empirical and longitudinal investigations in organizational contexts. The study also requires the decision framework to be implemented as a tool and to be integrated with the business rule software and systems specific to the organization. Given the time and tool development demands of the study, the evaluation was deemed outside the scope of this thesis and can be done as a future work. Another limitation is that the decision support system requires requisite inputs to process the recommendation, which includes the modeller's inputs of the characteristics of rules, the relevant process models, the modelling languages and systems being used, and other organizational settings. These inputs may not be readily available and some level of investment will be required by the organization to ensure that this information is visible and accessible to the users of the decision framework.

We foresee two extensions of our work. Firstly, as introduced in Chap. 2, Link is one of the three types of rule integration approaches, and the other two are text embedding and diagrammatic embedding. We selected rule linking in our experiment investigating the effect of rule linking on business process model understanding, and the effect of text embedding and diagrammatic embedding on business process model understanding are not evaluated yet. As introduced in Chap. 4, different integration approaches could affect the cognitive process of business process models differently in each of the four cognitive stages, and the effects are not evaluated. Secondly, as introduced in Chap. 7, an empirical evaluation of the decision framework in practice via case studies is needed to study the practical applicability of the decision framework.

# Appendix A: Online Survey

**Research Project Information Sheet**
Thank you for your interest in our study. This page provides you with information about our project, and your right in participating this survey. If at any time you wish to discuss the content of this survey, please feel free to contact us via the contact details below.

Project Title:
Evaluation of Factors Affecting Business Rule Modelling
Investigator:
Wei Wang
PhD Student, School of Information Technology and Electrical Engineering, University of Queensland
w.wang9@uq.edu.au

Supervisors:
Prof. Shazia Sadiq
School of Information Technology and Electrical Engineering, University of Queensland
shazia@itee.uq.edu.au
A/Prof. Marta Indulska
UQ Business School, University of Queensland
m.indulska@business.uq.edu.au

Expected duration:
The survey can take 15–30 min. However, there is NO time limit for any of the questions. You can spend as much time as you need.
The progress bar at the end of each page will indicate the progress of the survey. Questions starting with an asterisk (*) must be answered.

© Springer Nature Switzerland AG 2019
W. Wang, *Integrating Business Process Models and Rules*, LNBIP 343,
https://doi.org/10.1007/978-3-030-11809-9

Purpose of the project:
A business process is a collection of activities that takes one or more kinds of input and creates an output that is of value to the business. Business process modelling is a process of extracting, organizing and representing business activities to guide the analysis, implementation and to capture knowledge of business processes. Such structures also involve business rules, which describe constraints and requirements guiding and controlling the behaviour of business activities. Laws, regulations, policies and best practices are typical sources of business rules.

A business process can be represented as a process model, or as a set of business rules, or a combination of both. Whether a rule should be embedded into a business process model or modelled independently in a rule repository is an important question in the modelling of business processes. The study is focused on identifying and evaluating the factors that affect the decision of where to model business rules. Prior research has identified or implied several factors of business rules which may affect the placement of business rules, i.e. whether to model a business rule embedded in a business process or whether to model it independently using a business rule notation. We have identified these factors through a literature review and with this study we aim to evaluate the relative importance of these factors.

Your involvement:
In this study you will be given a questionnaire about factors that may affect modelling of business rules. You should rely on your knowledge and experience when answering these questions.

Details of participation:
Your involvement in the survey is voluntary and you have the right to stop the survey any time you wish during the session by exiting the survey system. You do not need to ask for permission to withdraw, nor give reasons for withdrawing. Should you withdraw from the study your data will be deleted.

Risks to you:
There are no risks to you participating in this study, beyond those that exist in normal everyday life.

Use of information:
All information provided by you will be used for this study and only serves the stated purpose of the study.

Confidentiality and privacy:
All personal data collected will be kept confidential prior to going through the de-identification process. No identifying information will be used in compiling the results of this research, and all information collected will be kept secure in an area of the School of Information Technology and Electrical Engineering network, so that it is properly backed up and preserved as per NHMRC/ARC guidelines. The information from the consent form, as well as the raw data collected will be kept confidential. In addition to the production of a PhD, the de-identified results of the study may be used for publication purposes in scientific journals and conferences.

This study adheres to the Guidelines of the ethical review process of The University of Queensland and the National Statement on Ethical Conduct in Human Research. You are free to discuss your participation in this study with one of the researchers involved in the project. Alternatively, if you would like to speak to an officer of the University not involved in the study, you may leave a message with the School Senior Administrative Officer - Research (rao@itee.uq.edu.au), for an ethics officer to contact you, or contact the University of Queensland Ethics Officer, Michael Tse, on 3365 3924, e-mail: humanethics@research.uq.edu.au.

**Participation Consent Form**

I have been provided with information about the procedure for evaluating factors affecting business rule modelling and I agree to take part. I understand that the study and the data are being used as part of a PhD research project. I understand that my participation is voluntary. I understand that I can withdraw from the study at any point for any reason. I understand that I will receive no benefit from this survey.

The handling of my data from this study has been explained to me. I understand that raw data collected is kept on a secured sever at the University of Queensland. I understand that data will not be shared with other people outside the project and that results from the data analysis will not reveal my identity.

Data collected will be analysed in private and its confidentiality will be maintained. This consent form will be stored separately from the data and will not be linked with the data in any way.

Researcher:
Wei Wang
School of Information Technology and Electrical Engineering
w.wang9@uq.edu.au
+61 7 33651186
Responsible UQ Staff Member:
Professor Shazia Sadiq
School of Information Technology and Electrical Engineering
shazia@itee.uq.edu.au
+61 7 3365 1999
Associate Professor Marta Indulska
UQ Business School
m.indulska@business.uq.edu.au
+61 7 3346 8034

I Agree
I Disagree

**The Survey**

Approximately, how many business process modelling notations or languages you have used?

O 0
O 1
O 2
O 3
O 4
O 5
O More than 5

Approximately, how many business rule modelling notations or languages you have used?

O 0
O 1
O 2
O 3
O 4
O 5
O More than 5

Approximately, how many years experience do you have in business process modelling overall?

O Less than 2 years
O Between 2 and 5 years
O Between 5 and 10
O Over 10 years

Approximately, how many years experience do you have in business rule modelling notations overall?

O None
O Less than 2 years
O Between 2 and 5 years
O Between 5 and 10
O Over 10 years

Approximately, how many business process models you have created over your working life?

O Less than 10 models
O Between 10 and 25 models
O Between 25 and 50 models
O Over 50 models

A business process can be represented as a process model, or as a set of business rules, or a combination of both. Whether a rule should be embedded into a business process model or modelled independently in a rule repository is an important question in the modelling of business processes. In the following, you will be asked to evaluate the 12 factors that have been identified through a literature review and may affect the decision of where to model business rules. Each factor will be defined and explained. You will be asked to indicate your opinions on the importance of the factor, its effect on the modelling of the business rule and which aspect(s) it will improve. Please consider each factor in isolation when answering the following questions.

Factor: Rate of Change
Description: Rate of Change refers to the frequency at which a business rule requires modification. Business rules can change in response to changes in regulations and policies.

How important is this factor in determining how a business rule should be modelled (i.e. embedded in a business process or modelled separately)?

- O 1 (Not at all important)
- O 2
- O 3
- O 4 (Neutral)
- O 5
- O 6
- O 7 (Very important)

Please indicate a reason for your judgement:
Considering two cases, one where rate of change is frequent, and second where rate of change is infrequent, where do you think a business rule should be modelled?

| | Embedded in a business process model | Independently as a business rule | I don't know |
|---|---|---|---|
| Frequent | O | O | O |
| Infrequent | O | O | O |

Factor: Accessibility
Description: Accessibility refers to the stakeholders' ability to view and manipulate a business rule. If a stakeholder can easily view or manipulate a rule in a format that is suitable to his or her need, then the rule has high accessibility, otherwise, the rule has low accessibility.

How important is this factor in determining how a business rule should be modelled
(i.e. embedded in a business process or modelled separately)?

    ○  1 (Not at all important)
    ○  2
    ○  3
    ○  4 (Neutral)
    ○  5
    ○  6
    ○  7 (Very important)

Please indicate a reason for your judgement:
Considering two cases, one where accessibility is high, and second where accessibility is low, where do you think a business rule should be modelled?

|  | Embedded in a business process model | Independently as a business rule | I don't know |
|---|---|---|---|
| High | ○ | ○ | ○ |
| Low | ○ | ○ | ○ |

Factor: Agility
Description: Agility refers to how quickly a business rule can be adapted to a
change. Rate of change deals with how frequently the rule needs to be changed, and
agility deals with how long will it take for each change to be modelled in a rule.

How important is this factor in determining how a business rule should be modelled
(i.e. embedded in a business process or modelled separately)?

    ○  1 (Not at all important)
    ○  2
    ○  3
    ○  4 (Neutral)
    ○  5
    ○  6
    ○  7 (Very important)

Please indicate a reason for your judgement:
Considering two cases, one where a rule can be adapted to a change quickly, and
second where the adaptation of a rule is slow, where do you think a business rule
should be modelled?

| | Embedded in a business process model | Independently as a business rule | I don't know |
|---|---|---|---|
| Quick | O | O | O |
| Slow | O | O | O |

Factor: Aspect of Change
Description: Aspect of Change refers to the component of the rule that can be changed. For example, the trigger condition of a rule, the reaction, the value of a parameter, and/or the whole logic of the rule. Depending on the component, the change might be simple or complex.

How important is this factor in determining how a business rule should be modelled (i.e. embedded in a business process or modelled separately)?

- O 1 (Not at all important)
- O 2
- O 3
- O 4 (Neutral)
- O 5
- O 6
- O 7 (Very important)

Please indicate a reason for your judgement:
Considering two cases, one where aspect of change is simple, and second where aspect of change is complex, where do you think a business rule should be modelled?

| | Embedded in a business process model | Independently as a business rule | I don't know |
|---|---|---|---|
| Simple | O | O | O |
| Complex | O | O | O |

Factor: Awareness of Impact

Description: Awareness of Impact refers to how well the implications of a business rule, or its changes, are understood. Some business rules have a direct and clear impact, while other rules may have an indirect or unclear impact. Thus, the impact may or may not be clear to the stakeholders.

How important is this factor in determining how a business rule should be modelled (i.e. embedded in a business process or modelled separately)?

- O  1 (Not at all important)
- O  2
- O  3
- O  4 (Neutral)
- O  5
- O  6
- O  7 (Very important)

Please indicate a reason for your judgement:

Considering two cases, one where impact is clear, and second where impact is unclear, where do you think a business rule should be modelled?

|         | Embedded in a business process model | Independently as a business rule | I don't know |
|---------|:---:|:---:|:---:|
| Clear   | O | O | O |
| Unclear | O | O | O |

Factor: Complexity

Description: Complexity refers to the level of difficulty in defining or understanding a business rule. Some rules are simple and some rules can be complex in nature.

How important is this factor in determining how a business rule should be modelled (i.e. embedded in a business process or modelled separately)?

- O  1 (Not at all important)
- O  2
- O  3
- O  4 (Neutral)
- O  5
- O  6
- O  7 (Very important)

Please indicate a reason for your judgement:
Considering two cases, one where a business rule is simple, and second where a business rule is complex, where do you think the business rule should be modelled?

| | Embedded in a business process model | Independently as a business rule | I don't know |
|---|---|---|---|
| Simple | O | O | O |
| Complex | O | O | O |

Factor: Criticality
Description: Criticality refers to the importance of the rule. Violation of critical rules can lead to severe consequences for the organization, while violation of non-critical rules may be less severe.

How important is this factor in determining how a business rule should be modelled (i.e. embedded in a business process or modelled separately)?

- O 1 (Not at all important)
- O 2
- O 3
- O 4 (Neutral)
- O 5
- O 6
- O 7 (Very important)

Please indicate a reason for your judgement:
Considering two cases, one where criticality is high, and second where criticality is low, where do you think a business rule should be modelled?

| | Embedded in a business process model | Independently as a business rule | I don't know |
|---|---|---|---|
| High | O | O | O |
| Low | O | O | O |

Factor: Governance Responsibility

Description: Governance refers to who ensures that business activities are in accordance with rules. Rules can be governed automatically by programs/systems, or manually by humans.

How important is this factor in determining how a business rule should be modelled (i.e. embedded in a business process or modelled separately)?

- O   1 (Not at all important)
- O   2
- O   3
- O   4 (Neutral)
- O   5
- O   6
- O   7 (Very important)

Please indicate a reason for your judgement:

Considering two cases, one where program is responsible for the governance, and second where human is responsible for the governance, where do you think a business rule should be modelled?

|                        | Embedded in a business process model | Independently as a business rule | I don't know |
|------------------------|:-----:|:-----:|:-----:|
| Automatic (Program)    |   O   |   O   |   O   |
| Manual (Human)         |   O   |   O   |   O   |

Factor: Implementation Responsibility

Description: Implementation Responsibility refers to who is charged with implementing or updating the business rule. Both business users and technical users could be responsible for the implementation of a business rule.

How important is this factor in determining how a business rule should be modelled (i.e. embedded in a business process or modelled separately)?

- O   1 (Not at all important)
- O   2
- O   3
- O   4 (Neutral)
- O   5
- O   6
- O   7 (Very important)

Please indicate a reason for your judgement:
Considering two cases, one where technical users are responsible for the implementation, and second where business users are responsible for the implementation, where do you think a business rule should be modelled?

| | Embedded in a business process model | Independently as a business rule | I don't know |
|---|---|---|---|
| Technical user | O | O | O |
| Business user | O | O | O |

Factor: Reusability
Description: Reusability refers to the potential for a rule to be used in new contexts. An existing business rule may be adapted or modified to fit new contexts and scenarios to reduce resources required in developing new rules.

How important is this factor in determining how a business rule should be modelled (i.e. embedded in a business process or modelled separately)?

O 1 (Not at all important)
O 2
O 3
O 4 (Neutral)
O 5
O 6
O 7 (Very important)

Please indicate a reason for your judgement:
Considering two cases, one where potential for reusability is high, and second where potential for reusability is low, where do you think a business rule should be modelled?

| | Embedded in a business process model | Independently as a business rule | I don't know |
|---|---|---|---|
| High | O | O | O |
| Low | O | O | O |

Factor: Rule Source
Description: Rule Source refers to the origin of the business rule. Rule sources could be external or internal – e.g. laws and regulations or internal policies and standards.

How important is this factor in determining how a business rule should be modelled (i.e. embedded in a business process or modelled separately)?

- O  1 (Not at all important)
- O  2
- O  3
- O  4 (Neutral)
- O  5
- O  6
- O  7 (Very important)

Please indicate a reason for your judgement:
Considering two cases, one where a business rule comes from an internal source, and second where a business rule comes from an external source, where do you think the business rule should be modelled?

|  | Embedded in a business process model | Independently as a business rule | I don't know |
|---|---|---|---|
| Internal | O | O | O |
| External | O | O | O |

Factor: Scope of Impact
Description: Scope of Impact refers the breadth of the impact of the rule. The impact of a business rule can be focused on an activity, an entire process, a department or the entire organization.

How important is this factor in determining how a business rule should be modelled (i.e. embedded in a business process or modelled separately)?

○  1 (Not at all important)
○  2
○  3
○  4 (Neutral)
○  5
○  6
○  7 (Very important)

Please indicate a reason for your judgement:
Considering two cases, one where the scope of impact is broad, and second where the scope of impact is limited, where do you think a business rule should be modelled?
Please rank the factors in descending order of importance. Drag at least 5 factors from the left and drop them to the box on the right. Use drag and drop in the box on the right to rank the selected factors.

| | Embedded in a business process model | Independently as a business rule | I don't know |
|---|---|---|---|
| Broad | ○ | ○ | ○ |
| Limited | ○ | ○ | ○ |

If there are other factors that you think are likely to affect where a business rule is modelled, please suggest them here and provide a brief explanation for your inclusion:

| Selected and Ranked Factors (at least 5) |
|---|
| Accessibility: the stakeholders' ability to view and manipulate a business rule |
| Agility: how quickly a business rule can be adapted to a change |
| Aspect of Change: the component of the rule that can be changed |
| Awareness of Impact: how well the implications of a business rule, or its changes, are understood |
| Complexity: the level of difficulty in defining or understanding a business rule |
| Criticality: the importance of the rule |
| Governance Responsibility: who ensures that business activities are in accordance with rules |
| Implementation Responsibility: who is charged with implementing or updating the business rule |
| Rate of Change: the frequency with which a business rule is to be modified |
| Reusability: the potential for a rule to be used in new contexts |
| Rule Source: the origin of the business rule |
| Scope of Impact: the breadth of the impact of the rule |

If you are interested in a summary of the results once the study is completed, please leave your email address to receive the result. Your email address:

Thank you for your participation!

# Appendix B: Experiment Materials

## Process 1

### Process Model

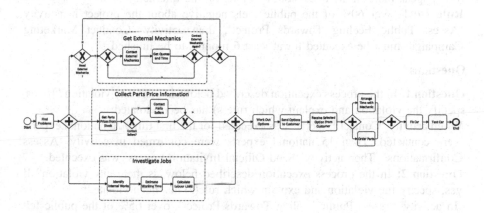

### Rules

**Rule 1:** At least 20 experts are required to be confirmed for this project, and the ratio between confirmed national and confirmed international experts should be greater than or equal to 2:1. Otherwise, activity group 'Select Experts' must be executed again.

W. Wang, *Integrating Business Process Models and Rules*, LNBIP 343,
https://doi.org/10.1007/978-3-030-11809-9

**Rule 2:** When activity 'Contact Experts' is executed for the first time, only national experts can be selected and contacted. If activity 'Contact Experts' is executed for the second or more times, both national and international experts can be contacted.
**Rule 3:** If activity group 'Select Experts' is executed for two or more times, the date for meeting shall be fixed at the same date as the previous date. If this is not possible, all selected experts shall be informed about the new meeting date, including experts who are contacted in previous executions of activity group 'Select Experts' but cannot confirm on the previously fixed date.
**Rule 4:** Construction cost is a one-off cost and cannot exceed 3 billion.
**Rule 5:** Operating cost is limited to 2 billion for the entire project. Operating cost per year cannot exceed 10% of operating cost for the entire project.
**Rule 6:** Operating cost for the entire project cannot exceed 50% of the total budget.
**Rule 7:** In activity "Assess Public Feeling Towards Project", a survey with at least 500 participants must be carried out to assess public feeling towards the project.
**Rule 8:** If over 30% of the public feels negative about the project in activity 'Assess Public Feeling Towards Project', then activity 'Find Marketing Firm' needs to be executed.
**Rule 9:** In activity "Define Marketing Plan", the marketing plan includes plan on newspapers, plan on the television, and plan on the Internet.
**Rule 10:** If over 60% of the public feels negative about the project in activity 'Assess Public Feeling Towards Project', then activity 'Conduct Marketing Campaign' must be executed for at least 6 months to be finished.

## Questions

**Question 1:** In the process execution described below, is there any violation? If yes, specify the violation and explain which rule(s) has been violated:
When activity 'Contact Experts' was executed for the first time, 20 national experts were contacted. Then 15 national experts were confirmed in activity 'Assess Confirmations'. Then activity 'Send Official Invitation Letters' was executed.
**Question 2:** In the process execution described below, is there any violation? If yes, specify the violation and explain which rule(s) has been violated:
In activity 'Assess Public Feeling Towards Project', over 65% of the public felt negative about the project. Activity 'Conduct Marketing Campaign' was started in January, and was finished 4 months later after being started. Then activity 'Inform Experts about the Project' was executed.
**Question 3:** In the process execution described below, is there any violation? If yes, specify the violation and explain which rule(s) has been violated:
As the result of the execution of activity group 'Define Financial Cost', total budget for this project is 3 billion, construction cost is 1 billion, operating cost is 2 billion for the entire project, and operating cost per year is 0.2 billion.

# Process 2

## Process Model

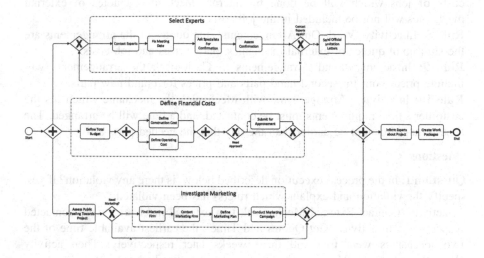

## Rules

**Rule 1:** In activity 'Investigate Car', if there is any problem that can only be fixed by external mechanics, then activity group 'Investigate External Mechanics' must be executed.

**Rule 2:** Two special mechanics need to be contacted in activity 'Contact External Mechanics', and in activity 'Get Quotes and Time', at least one of the external mechanics is available in the following two weeks. Otherwise, activity group 'Investigate External Mechanics' must be executed again.

**Rule 3:** In activity group "Investigate Parts", both price of a second-hand part and price of a brand-new part must be collected.

**Rule 4:** If in activity 'Check Storage', a part needed is not in stock, then in activity 'Get Parts Prices', the part should have a price for brand new one, and a price for second hand one.

**Rule 5:** If in activity 'Check Storage', a second hand part is in stock, then in activity 'Get Parts Prices', only the price for a brand new one is needed. If in activity 'Check Storage', a brand new part is in stock, then in activity 'Get Parts Prices', only the price for a second hand one is needed.

**Rule 6:** In activity 'Identify Jobs', only the jobs that will be done by internal mechanics need to be identified.

**Rule 7:** In activity 'Calculate Job Costs', job costs are calculated as the sum of the costs of jobs which will be done by internal mechanics. Quotes of external mechanics will not be included in the job costs.

**Rule 8:** In activity 'Work Out Arrangements', the quotes in the arrangements are the sum up of quotes of external mechanics, parts prices and job costs.

**Rule 9:** In activity 'Send Arrangements to Customer', the arrangements will include prices both for second hand parts and prices for brand new parts.

**Rule 10:** In activity 'Arrange Time with Mechanic', the mechanic which fits the customer's time requirements must be contacted, and a time will be arranged. The time arranged cannot be earlier than the day that the needed parts arrive.

### Questions

**Question 1:** In the process execution described below, is there any violation? If yes, specify the violation and explain which rule(s) has been violated:
In activity 'Contact External Mechanics', two external mechanics were contacted respectively. In activity 'Get Quotes and Time', the earliest available time of the two mechanics were two and three weeks later respectively. Then activity 'Investigate External Mechanics' was considered as finished.

**Question 2:** In the process execution described below, is there any violation? If yes, specify the violation and explain which rule(s) has been violated:
In activity group "Investigate Parts", a car needed two parts to be fixed: part A and part B. In activity 'Check Storage', a second-hand part A is in stock. Then activity 'Contact Part Sellers' was executed. Then in activity 'Get Parts Prices', the prices for a second-hand part B were collected. Then activity group 'Investigate Parts' was considered finished.

**Question 3:** In the process execution described below, is there any violation? If yes, specify the violation and explain which rule(s) has been violated:
In activity 'Identify Jobs', two local jobs Job1 and Job2 were identified, and the costs were $500 for each of the two jobs. In activity 'Get Quotes and Time', the quote of external mechanics was $300. Then in activity 'Calculate Job Costs', the job costs were calculated as $1300.

# References

1. Hammer, M., Champy, J.: Reengineering the corporation: a manifesto for business revolution. Bus. Horiz. **36**, 90–91 (1993)
2. Kovacic, A., Groznik, A.: The business rule-transformation approach. Presented at the 26th International Conference on Information Technology Interfaces, June 2004
3. Knolmayer, G., Endl, R., Pfahrer, M.: Modelling processes and workflows by business rules. In: van der Aalst, W., Desel, J., Oberweis, A. (eds.) Business Process Management. LNCS, pp. 16–29. Springer, Heidelberg (2000). https://doi.org/10.1007/3 540-45594-9_2
4. Nayak, N., et al.: Core business architecture for a service-oriented enterprise. IBM Syst. J. **46**, 723–742 (2007)
5. Zur Muehlen, M., Indulska, M.: Modelling languages for business processes and business rules: a representational analysis. Inf. Syst. **35**, 379–390 (2010)
6. Recker, J., Rosemann, M., Green, P.F., Indulska, M.: Do ontological deficiencies in modelling grammars matter? MIS Q. **35**, 57–79 (2011)
7. Nemuraite, L., Skersys, T., Sukys, A., Sinkevicius, E., Ablonskis, L.: VETIS tool for editing and transforming SBVR business vocabularies and business rules into UML&OCL models. In: 16th International Conference on Information and Software Technologies, pp. 377–384. Kaunas University of Technology, Kaunas (2010)
8. Zur Muehlen, M., Indulska, M., Kittel, K.: Towards integrated modelling of business processes and business rules. In: Proceedings of the 19th Australasian Conference on Information Systems, pp. 690–697. Springer, Heidelberg (2008)
9. Skersys, T., Tutkute, L., Butleris, R., Butkiene, R.: Extending BPMN business process model with SBVR business vocabulary and rules. Inf. Technol. Control **41**, 356–367 (2012)
10. Rabova, I.: Methodology of the enterprise architecture creating and the role of the enterprise architecture in rural development. Agric. Econ.-Zemedelska Ekonomika **56**, 334–340 (2010)
11. Cheng, R., Sadiq, S., Indulska, M.: Framework for business process and rule integration: a case of BPMN and SBVR. In: Abramowicz, W. (ed.) International Conference on Business Information Systems. LNCS, vol. 87, pp. 13–24. Springer, Heidelberg (2011). https://doi.org/10.1007/978-3-642-21863-7_2
12. Ly, L.T., Rinderle-Ma, S., Göser, K., Dadam, P.: On enabling integrated process compliance with semantic constraints in process management systems. Inf. Syst. Front. **14**, 195–219 (2012)
13. Green, P., Indulska, M., Recker, J., Rosemann, M.: Do process modelling techniques get better? A comparative ontological analysis of BPMN. In: ACIS 2005 Proceedings, pp. 36–47. Springer, Heidelberg (2005)

© Springer Nature Switzerland AG 2019
W. Wang, *Integrating Business Process Models and Rules*, LNBIP 343,
https://doi.org/10.1007/978-3-030-11809-9

14. Green, P.F., Rosemann, M.: Perceived ontological weaknesses of process modelling techniques: further evidence. In: ECIS, pp. 312–321 (2002)

15. Habich, D., et al.: Joining business rules and business processes. In: Proceedings of IT, pp. 1–12 (2010)

16. Recker, J., Indulska, M., Rosemann, M., Green, P.: The ontological deficiencies of process modelling in practice. Eur. J. Inf. Syst. **19**, 501–525 (2010)

17. Wang, W., Indulska, M., Sadiq, S.: Integrated modelling of business process models and business rules: a research agenda. In: Proceedings of the 25th Australasian Conference on Information Systems (ACIS). University of Auckland Business School, Auckland (2014)

18. Sapkota, B., van Sinderen, M.: Exploiting rules and processes for increasing flexibility in service composition. In: 14th IEEE International Conference on Enterprise Distributed Object Computing Conference Workshops (EDOCW), pp. 177–185. IEEE (2010)

19. Kluza, K., Kaczor, K., Nalepa, G.J.: Enriching business processes with rules using the Oryx BPMN editor. In: Rutkowski, L., Korytkowski, M., Scherer, R., Tadeusiewicz, R., Zadeh, L.A., Zurada, J.M. (eds.) Artificial Intelligence and Soft Computing, Pt Ii. pp. 573–581 (2012)

20. Nalepa, G.J., Kluza, K., Kaczor, K.: Proposal of an inference engine architecture for business rules and processes. In: Rutkowski, L., Korytkowski, M., Scherer, R., Tadeusiewicz, R., Zadeh, L.A., Zurada, J.M. (eds.) ICAISC 2013. LNCS (LNAI), vol. 7895, pp. 453–464. Springer, Heidelberg (2013). https://doi.org/10.1007/978-3-642-38610-7_42

21. Milanovic, M., Gasevic, D., Rocha, L.: Modelling flexible business processes with business rule patterns. Presented at the 15th IEEE International Conference on Enterprise Distributed Object Computing Conference (EDOC), August 2011

22. Governatori, G., Shek, S.: Rule based business process compliance. In: Proceedings of the RuleML, pp. 5–6 (2012)

23. Kappel, G., Rausch-Schott, S., Retschitzegger, W.: Coordination in workflow management systems—a rule-based approach. In: Conen, W., Neumann, G. (eds.) ASIAN 1996. LNCS, vol. 1364, pp. 99–119. Springer, Heidelberg (1998). https://doi.org/10.1007/BFb0027102

24. PNMSOFT: Business Process Management Life Cycle. http://www.pnmsoft.com/resources/bpm-tutorial/bpm-lifecycle/

25. Lu, R., Sadiq, S.: A survey of comparative business process modelling approaches. Presented at the International Conference on Business Information Systems (2007)

26. Recker, J., Indulska, M., zur Muehlen, M., Green, P.: How good is BPMN really? Insights from theory and practice. In: Proceedings on the 14th European Conference on Information Systems, Göteborg, Sweden, pp. 31–46 (2006)

27. OMG: BPMN 2.0 by Example. http://www.omg.org/cgi-bin/doc?dtc/10-06-02.pdf

28. UML Activity Diagram Examples. http://www.uml-diagrams.org/activity-diagrams-examples.html

29. Event-Driven Process Chain (EPC). http://www.ariscommunity.com/event-driven-process-chain

30. Event-Driven Process Chains – Overview. http://download.arcway.net/online-help/cockpit-enterprise-client_3-4-0/index.jsp?topic=%2Fcom.arcway.planagent.planmodel.bpre.epc%2Fhelp%2Fcontent%2Fbpre%2Fepc%2Findex.html

31. Peterson, J.L.: Petri Net Theory and the Modelling of Systems (1981)

32. Al-Fedaghi, S., Alloughani, R., Al Sanousi, M.: A new methodology for process modelling of workflows. J. Softw. Eng. Appl. **5**, 560–567 (2012)

33. Burton-Jones, A., Meso, P.N.: Conceptualizing systems for understanding: an empirical test of decomposition principles in object-oriented analysis. Inf. Syst. Res. **17**, 38–60 (2006)

34. Scaife, M., Rogers, Y.: External cognition: how do graphical representations work? Int. J. Hum.-Comput. Stud. **45**, 185–213 (1996)

35. Larkin, J.H., Simon, H.A.: Why a diagram is (sometimes) worth ten thousand words. Cogn. Sci. **11**, 65–100 (1987)

36. Embley, D.W., Thalheim, B.: Handbook of Conceptual Modelling. Springer, Heidelberg (2014). https://doi.org/10.1007/978-3-642-15865-0

37. Burton-Jones, A., Meso, P.N.: The effects of decomposition quality and multiple forms of information on novices' understanding of a domain from a conceptual model. J. Assoc. Inf. Syst. **9**, 748–802 (2008)

38. Wand, Y., Weber, R.: An ontological model of an information system. IEEE Trans. Softw. Eng. **16**, 1282–1292 (1990)

39. Burton-Jones, A., Clarke, R., Lazarenko, K., Weber, R.: Is use of optional attributes and associations in conceptual modelling always problematic? Theory and empirical tests. In: 33rd International Conference on Information Systems (ICIS 2012), pp. 1–16. Association for Information Systems (2012)

40. Bunge, M.: Treatise on Basic Philosophy: Ontology I: the Furniture of the World. Springer, Dordrecht (1977). https://doi.org/10.1007/978-94-010-9924-0

41. Wand, Y., Weber, R.: On the ontological expressiveness of information systems analysis and design grammars. Inf. Syst. J. **3**, 217–237 (1993)

42. Allen, G.N., March, S.T.: The effects of state-based and event-based data representation on user performance in query formulation tasks. MIS Q. **30**, 269–290 (2006)

43. Bodart, F., Patel, A., Sim, M., Weber, R.: Should optional properties be used in conceptual modelling? A theory and three empirical tests. Inf. Syst. Res. **12**, 384–405 (2001)

44. Shanks, G., Tansley, E., Nuredini, J., Tobin, D., Weber, R.: Representing part-whole relationships in conceptual modelling: an empirical evaluation. In: ICIS 2002 Proceedings, pp. 9–24 (2002)

45. Reijers, H.A., Mendling, J., Dijkman, R.M.: Human and automatic modularizations of process models to enhance their comprehension. Inf. Syst. **36**, 881–897 (2011)

46. Turetken, O., Rompen, T., Vanderfeesten, I., Dikici, A., van Moll, J.: The effect of modularity representation and presentation medium on the understandability of business process models in BPMN. In: La Rosa, M., Loos, P., Pastor, O. (eds.) BPM 2016. LNCS, vol. 9850, pp. 289–307. Springer, Cham (2016). https://doi.org/10.1007/978-3-319-45348-4_17

47. La Rosa, M., Ter Hofstede, A.H., Wohed, P., Reijers, H.A., Mendling, J., van der Aalst, W. M.: Managing process model complexity via concrete syntax modifications. IEEE Trans. Ind. Inform. **7**, 255–265 (2011)

48. Johannsen, F., Leist, S., Braunnagel, D.: Testing the impact of Wand and Weber's decomposition model on process model understandability (2014)

49. Zugal, S., Pinggera, J., Weber, B., Mendling, J., Reijers, H.A.: Assessing the impact of hierarchy on model understandability – a cognitive perspective. In: Kienzle, J. (ed.) MODELS 2011. LNCS, vol. 7167, pp. 123–133. Springer, Heidelberg (2012). https://doi.org/10.1007/978-3-642-29645-1_14

50. Mendling, J., Strembeck, M., Recker, J.: Factors of process model comprehension—findings from a series of experiments. Decis. Support Syst. **53**, 195–206 (2012)

51. Recker, J.: Empirical investigation of the usefulness of gateway constructs in process models. Eur. J. Inf. Syst. **22**, 673–689 (2012)

52. Aguilar, E.R., García, F., Ruiz, F., Piattini, M., Visaggio, C.A., Canfora, G.: Evaluation of BPMN models quality-a family of experiments. In: ENASE, pp. 56–63 (2008)

53. Sánchez-González, L., García, F., Mendling, J., Ruiz, F.: Quality assessment of business process models based on thresholds. In: Meersman, R., Dillon, T., Herrero, P. (eds.) OTM 2010. LNCS, vol. 6426, pp. 78–95. Springer, Heidelberg (2010). https://doi.org/10.1007/978-3-642-16934-2_9

54. Figl, K., Laue, R.: Influence factors for local comprehensibility of process models. Int. J. Hum.-Comput. Stud. **82**, 96–110 (2015)

55. Mendling, J., Strembeck, M.: Influence factors of understanding business process models. In: Abramowicz, W., Fensel, D. (eds.) BIS 2008. LNBIP, vol. 7, pp. 142–153. Springer, Heidelberg (2008). https://doi.org/10.1007/978-3-540-79396-0_13

56. Gruhn, V., Laue, R.: Adopting the cognitive complexity measure for business process models. Presented at the 5th IEEE International Conference on Cognitive Informatics (2006)

57. Kummer, T.-F., Recker, J., Mendling, J.: Enhancing understandability of process models through cultural-dependent color adjustments. Decis. Support Syst. **87**, 1–12 (2016)

58. Mendling, J., Reijers, H.A., Recker, J.: Activity labeling in process modelling: Empirical insights and recommendations. Inf. Syst. **35**, 467–482 (2010)

59. Bera, P.: Does cognitive overload matter in understanding BPMN models? J. Comput. Inf. Syst. **52**, 59–69 (2012)

60. Figl, K., Recker, J., Mendling, J.: A study on the effects of routing symbol design on process model comprehension. Decis. Support Syst. **54**, 1104–1118 (2013)

61. Recker, J.C., Dreiling, A.: Does it matter which process modelling language we teach or use? An experimental study on understanding process modelling languages without formal education. Presented at the 18th Australasian Conference on Information Systems, Toowoomba, Australia (2007)

62. Recker, J., Reijers, H.A., van de Wouw, S.G.: Process model comprehension: the effects of cognitive abilities, learning style, and strategy. Commun. Assoc. Inf. Syst. **34**, 199–222 (2014)

63. Weitlaner, D., Guettinger, A., Kohlbacher, M.: Intuitive comprehensibility of process models. In: Fischer, H., Schneeberger, J. (eds.) S-BPM ONE 2013. CCIS, vol. 360, pp. 52–71. Springer, Heidelberg (2013). https://doi.org/10.1007/978-3-642-36754-0_4

64. Figl, K., Recker, J.: Exploring cognitive style and task-specific preferences for process representations. Requirements Eng. **21**, 63–85 (2016)

65. Reijers, H.A., Mendling, J.: A study into the factors that influence the understandability of business process models. IEEE Trans. Syst. Man Cybern. Part A: Syst. Hum. **41**, 449–462 (2011)

66. Ceri, S.: Designing Database Applications with Objects and Rules: The IDEA Methodology. Addison Wesley, Boston (1997)

67. Hay, D., Healy, K.A., Hall, J.: Defining business rules-what are they really (2000)

68. Selfridge, P.G., Waters, R.C., Chikofsky, E.J.: Challenges to the field of reverse engineering. In: Proceedings of Working Conference on Reverse Engineering, pp. 144–150. IEEE (1993)

69. Rosca, D., Greenspan, S., Feblowitz, M., Wild, C.: A decision making methodology in support of the business rules lifecycle. In: Proceedings of the Third IEEE International Symposium on Requirements Engineering, pp. 236–246. IEEE (1997)

70. do Prado Leite, J.C.S., Leonardi, M.C.: Business rules as organizational policies. Presented at the Ninth International Workshop on Software Specification and Design, April 1998

71. Giblin, C., Müller, S., Pfitzmann, B.: From regulatory policies to event monitoring rules: towards model-driven compliance automation. IBM Research Zurich, Report RZ 3662 (2006)

72. Sasaki, H.: Intelligent and Knowledge-Based Computing for Business and Organizational Advancements. IGI Global, Hershey (2012)

73. Wagner, G.: Rule modeling and markup. In: Eisinger, N., Małuszyński, J. (eds.) Reasoning Web. LNCS, vol. 3564, pp. 251–274. Springer, Heidelberg (2005). https://doi.org/10.1007/11526988_7

74. Integrity Rules in R2ML. https://oxygen.informatik.tu-cottbus.de/rewerse-i1/?q=constraints

75. Weber, R.: Ontological foundations of information systems. Coopers & Lybrand and the Accounting Association of Australia and New Zealand, Melbourne (1997)

76. Krogstie, J., McBrien, P., Owens, R., Seltveit, A.H.: Information systems development using a combination of process and rule based approaches. In: Andersen, R., Bubenko, J.A., Sølvberg, A. (eds.) CAiSE 1991. LNCS, vol. 498, pp. 319–335. Springer, Heidelberg (1991). https://doi.org/10.1007/3-540-54059-8_92

77.  McBrien, P., Seltveit, A.H.: Coupling process models and business rules. In: Sölvberg, A., Krogstie, J., Seltveit, A.H. (eds.) Information Systems Development for Decentralized Organizations. ITIFIP, pp. 201–217. Springer, Boston (1995). https://doi.org/10.1007/978-0-387-34871-1_12

78.  Meng, J., Su, S.Y., Lam, H., Helal, A.: Achieving dynamic inter-organizational workflow management by integrating business processes, events and rules. In: Proceedings of the 35th Annual Hawaii International Conference on System Sciences, pp. 10–29. IEEE (2002)

79.  Nalepa, G.J.: Proposal of business process and rules modelling with the XTT method. In: Proceedings of the Ninth International Symposium on Symbolic and Numeric Algorithms for Scientific Computing, pp. 500–506. IEEE Computer Society, Washington, DC (2007)

80.  Rabova, I.: Business rules specification and business processes modelling. Agric. Econ.-Zemedelska Ekonomika **55**, 20–24 (2009)

81.  Skersys, T., Tutkute, L., Butleris, R.: The enrichment of BPMN business process model with SBVR business vocabulary and rules. J. Comput. Inf. Technol. **20**, 143–150 (2012)

82.  Sadiq, S., Governatori, G., Namiri, K.: Modeling control objectives for business process compliance. In: Alonso, G., Dadam, P., Rosemann, M. (eds.) BPM 2007. LNCS, vol. 4714, pp. 149–164. Springer, Heidelberg (2007). https://doi.org/10.1007/978-3-540-75183-0_12

83.  Boukhebouze, M., Amghar, Y., Benharkat, A.-N., Maamar, Z.: A rule-based modeling for the description of flexible and self-healing business processes. In: Grundspenkis, J., Morzy, T., Vossen, G. (eds.) ADBIS 2009. LNCS, vol. 5739, pp. 15–27. Springer, Heidelberg (2009). https://doi.org/10.1007/978-3-642-03973-7_3

84.  Zhao, K., Ying, S., Zhang, L., Hu, L.: Achieving business process and business rules integration using SPL. In: 2010 International Conference on Future Information Technology and Management Engineering (FITME), pp. 329–332 (2010)

85.  Di Bona, D., Lo Re, G., Aiello, G., Tamburo, A., Alessi, M.: A methodology for graphical modelling of business rules. In: Proceedings of the 5th European Symposium on Computer Modelling and Simulation, Madrid, Spain, pp. 102–106 (2011)

86.  Peffers, K., Tuunanen, T., Rothenberger, M.A., Chatterjee, S.: A design science research methodology for information systems research. J. Manag. Inf. Syst. **24**, 45–77 (2007)

87.  von Alan, R.H., March, S.T., Park, J., Ram, S.: Design science in information systems research. MIS Q. **28**, 75–105 (2004)

88.  Guthrie, J.T.: Locating information in documents: examination of a cognitive model. Read. Res. Q. **23**, 178–199 (1988)

89.  Gregor, S.: The nature of theory in information systems. MIS Q. **30**, 611–642 (2006)

90.  Atkinson, R.C., Shiffrin, R.M.: Human memory: a proposed system and its control processes. Psychol. Learn. Motiv. **2**, 89–195 (1968)

91.  Sweller, J.: Cognitive load during problem solving: effects on learning. Cogn. Sci. **12**, 257–285 (1988)

92.  Paas, F., Tuovinen, J.E., Tabbers, H., Gerven, P.W.M.V.: Cognitive load measurement as a means to advance cognitive load theory. Educ. Psychol. **38**, 63–71 (2003)

93.  Paas, F.G., Van Merriënboer, J.J.: Instructional control of cognitive load in the training of complex cognitive tasks. Educ. Psychol. Rev. **6**, 351–371 (1994)

94.  Bera, P., Burton-Jones, A., Wand, Y.: Guidelines for designing visual ontologies to support knowledge identification. MIS Q. **35**, 883–908 (2011)

95.  Bowen, P.L., O'Farrell, R.A., Rohde, F.H.: Analysis of competing data structures: does ontological clarity produce better end user query performance. J. Assoc. Inf. Syst. **7**, 22 (2006)

96.  Vessey, I.: Cognitive fit: a theory-based analysis of the graphs versus tables literature. Decis. Sci. **22**, 219–240 (1991)

97.  Chandler, P., Sweller, J.: The split-attention effect as a factor in the design of instruction. Br. J. Educ. Psychol. **62**, 233–246 (1992)

98.  Chandler, P., Sweller, J.: Cognitive load theory and the format of instruction. Cogn. Instr. **8**, 293–332 (1991)

99. Kalyuga, S., Chandler, P., Sweller, J.: Managing split-attention and redundancy in multimedia instruction. Appl. Cogn. Psychol. **13**, 351–371 (1999)

100. Sweller, J., Chandler, P.: Why some material is difficult to learn. Cogn. Instr. **12**, 185–233 (1994)

101. Sperber, D., Wilson, D., He, Z., Ran, Y.: Relevance: Communication and Cognition. Harvard University Press, Cambridge (1986)

102. Blackwell, A., Green, T.: Notational systems–the cognitive dimensions of notations framework. In: HCI Models, Theories, and Frameworks: Toward an Interdisciplinary Science. Morgan Kaufmann, Burlington (2003)

103. Loucopoulos, P., Kadir, W.M.N.W.: BROOD: business rules-driven object oriented design. J. Database Manag. (JDM) **19**, 41–73 (2008)

104. Wang, W., Indulska, M., Sadiq, S.: Cognitive efforts in using integrated models of business processes and rules - semantic scholar. In: Proceedings of the 28th International Conference on Advanced Information Systems Engineering (CAiSE Workshop), pp. 20–35. Springer, Ljubljana (2016)

105. Charness, G., Gneezy, U., Kuhn, M.A.: Experimental methods: between-subject and within-subject design. J. Econ. Behav. Organ. **81**, 1–8 (2012)

106. Meghanathan, R.N., van Leeuwen, C., Nikolaev, A.R.: Fixation duration surpasses pupil size as a measure of memory load in free viewing. Front. Hum. Neurosci. **8**, 1063–1080 (2015)

107. Haji, F.A., Rojas, D., Childs, R., de Ribaupierre, S., Dubrowski, A.: Measuring cognitive load: performance, mental effort and simulation task complexity. Med. Educ. **49**, 815–827 (2015)

108. Zugal, S.: Applying Cognitive Psychology for Improving the Creation, Understanding and Maintenance of Business Process Models (2013)

109. Gruhn, V., Laue, R.: Complexity metrics for business process models. In: 9th International Conference on Business Information Systems, pp. 1–12 (2006)

110. Labovitz, S.: Criteria for selecting a significance level: a note on the sacredness of 05. Am. Sociol. **3**, 220–222 (1968)

111. Wang, W., Indulska, M., Sadiq, S.: Factors affecting business process and business rule integration. In: Proceedings of the 25th Australasian Conference on Information Systems (ACIS), pp. 30–45. University of Auckland Business School, Auckland (2014)

112. Davies, I., Green, P., Rosemann, M., Indulska, M., Gallo, S.: How do practitioners use conceptual modelling in practice? Data Knowl. Eng. **58**, 358–380 (2006)

113. Wallace, R.O., Mellor, C.J.: Nonresponse bias in mail accounting surveys: a pedagogical note. Br. Acc. Rev. **20**, 131–139 (1988)

114. Malhotra, N.K.: Marketing Research: An Applied Orientation, 5th edn. Pearson Education India, New Delhi (2008)

115. Kim, J.W., Jain, R.: Web services composition with traceability centered on dependency. In: Proceedings of the 38th Annual Hawaii International Conference on System Sciences, p. 89. IEEE (2005)

116. van Roosmalen, M.W., Hoppenbrouwers, S.: Supporting corporate governance with enterprise architecture and business rule management: a synthesis of stability and agility. In: Proceedings of the International Workshop on Regulations Modelling and Deployment, pp. 20–35 (2008)

117. Taveter, K., Wagner, G.: Agent-oriented enterprise modeling based on business rules. In: S. Kunii, H., Jajodia, S., Sølvberg, A. (eds.) ER 2001. LNCS, vol. 2224, pp. 527–540. Springer, Heidelberg (2001). https://doi.org/10.1007/3-540-45581-7_39

118. Kontopoulos, E., Bassiliades, N., Antoniou, G.: Deploying defeasible logic rule bases for the semantic web. Data Knowl. Eng. **66**, 116–146 (2008)

119. Iwaihara, M., Shiga, T., Kozawa, M.: Extracting business rules from web product descriptions. In: Zhou, X., Su, S., Papazoglou, M.P., Orlowska, M.E., Jeffery, K. (eds.) WISE 2004. LNCS, vol. 3306, pp. 135–146. Springer, Heidelberg (2004). https://doi.org/10.1007/978-3-540-30480-7_15

120. Moreira, A., Fiadeiro, J.L., Andrade, L.: Evolving requirements through coordination contracts. In: Eder, J., Missikoff, M. (eds.) CAiSE 2003. LNCS, vol. 2681, pp. 633–646. Springer, Heidelberg (2003). https://doi.org/10.1007/3-540-45017-3_42

121. Nelson, M.L., Peterson, J., Rariden, R.L., Sen, R.: Transitioning to a business rule management service model: Case studies from the property and casualty insurance industry. Inf. Manag. **47**, 30–41 (2010)

122. Mammar, A., Ramel, S., Grégoire, B., Schmitt, M., Guelfi, N.: Efficient: a toolset for building trusted B2B transactions. In: Pastor, O., Falcão e Cunha, J. (eds.) CAiSE 2005. LNCS, vol. 3520, pp. 430–445. Springer, Heidelberg (2005). https://doi.org/10.1007/11431855_30

123. Zhang, C., Meservy, T.O., Lee, E.T., Dhaliwal, J.: An exploratory case study of the benefits of business rules management systems. In: ICIS 2009 Proceedings, pp. 19–34 (2009)

124. Ram, S., Khatri, V.: A comprehensive framework for modelling set-based business rules during conceptual database design. Inf. Syst. **30**, 89–118 (2005)

125. Fu, G., Shao, J., Embury, S.M., Gray, W.A.: Algorithms for analysing related constraint business rules. Data Knowl. Eng. **50**, 215–240 (2004)

126. Wang, J., Rosca, D.: Dynamic workflow modeling and verification. In: Dubois, E., Pohl, K. (eds.) CAiSE 2006. LNCS, vol. 4001, pp. 303–318. Springer, Heidelberg (2006). https://doi.org/10.1007/11767138_21

127. Moody, D.L.: Measuring the quality of data models: an empirical evaluation of the use of quality metrics in practice. In: European Conference on Information Systems, pp. 78–88 (2003)

128. Krogh, E., El Sawy, O.A., Gray, P.: Managing online in perpetual perfect storms: insights from indymac bank. MIS Q. Exec. **4**, 425–442 (2005)

129. Srivastava, S.C., Mathur, S.S., Teo, T.S.H.: Modernization of passenger reservation system: Indian Railways' dilemma. J. Inf. Technol. **22**, 432–439 (2007)

130. Cappelli, C., Santoro, F.M., Leite, J.C.S.P., Batista, T., Medeiros, A.L., Romeiro, C.S.C.: Reflections on the modularity of business process models: the case for introducing the aspect-oriented paradigm. Bus. Process Manag. J. **16**, 662–687 (2010)

131. Weigand, H., van den Heuvel, W.-J., Hiel, M.: Rule-based service composition and service-oriented business rule management. In: Proceedings of the International Workshop on Regulations Modelling and Deployment (ReMoD 2008), pp. 1–12. Citeseer (2008)

132. Witman, P.D.: Software product lines and configurable product bases in business applications-a case from financial services. In: 42nd Hawaii International Conference on System Sciences, HICSS 2009, pp. 1–10. IEEE (2009)

133. Johnstone, M.N., McDermid, D.C., Venable, J.R.: Teaching an old dog new tricks: modelling electronic commerce with business rules. In: Proceedings of the 11th Australasian Conference on Information Systems (2000)

134. Karami, N., Iijima, J.: A dynamic knowledge approach for dynamic business rules modelling. In: Proceedings of PACIS 2006, pp. 96–101 (2006)

135. Halpin, T.: Augmenting UML with fact-orientation. Presented at the 34th Annual Hawaii International Conference on System Sciences (2001)

136. Currim, F., Ram, S.: Conceptually modelling windows and bounds for space and time in database constraints. Commun. ACM **51**, 125–129 (2008)

137. Currim, F., Ram, S.: Modelling spatial and temporal set-based constraints during conceptual database design. Inf. Syst. Res. **23**, 109–128 (2012)

138. Iyer, B., Freedman, J., Gaynor, M., Wyner, G.: Web services: enabling dynamic business networks. Commun. Assoc. Inf. Syst. **11**, 38 (2003)

139. Dullea, J., Song, I.-Y., Lamprou, I.: An analysis of structural validity in entity-relationship modelling. Data Knowl. Eng. **47**, 167–205 (2003)

140. Stirna, J., Persson, A., Sandkuhl, K.: Participative enterprise modeling: experiences and recommendations. In: Krogstie, J., Opdahl, A., Sindre, G. (eds.) CAiSE 2007. LNCS, vol. 4495, pp. 546–560. Springer, Heidelberg (2007). https://doi.org/10.1007/978-3-540-72988-4_38

141. Berger, H., Beynon-Davies, P., Cleary, P.: The utility of a rapid application development (RAD) approach for a large complex information Systems development. In: ECIS 2004 Proceedings, p. 7 (2004)

142. Lee, S.H., Haider, A., Kim, J.G., Bahador, K.M.K.: Information quality assessment in Korean manufacturing organization. In: Proceedings of the 23rd Australasian Conference on Information Systems, pp. 1–11. ACIS (2012)

143. Ofner, M.H., Otto, B., Österle, H.: Integrating a data quality perspective into business process management. Bus. Process Manag. J. **18**, 1036–1067 (2012)

144. Otto, B., Ebner, V., Hüner, K.: Measuring master data quality: findings from a case study. In: Proceedings of AMCIS 2010, pp. 10–21 (2010)

145. Neely, M.P., Lin, S., Gao, J., Koronios, A.: The deficiencies of current data quality tools in the realm of engineering asset management. In: Proceedings of the Twelfth Americas Conference in Information Systems, pp. 59–70 (2006)

146. Green, P., Rosemann, M., Ipswich, A.: Ontological analysis of integrated process models: testing hypotheses. Aust. J. Inf. Syst. **9**, 30–38 (2001)

147. Ho, D.T.-Y., zur Muehlen, M.: From the stone age to the cloud: a case study of risk-focused process improvement. In: Proceedings of Australasian Conference on Computer and Information Science, Shanghai, China, pp. 144–160 (2009)

148. Meersman, D., De Leenheer, P., Hadzic, F.: Patient and business rules extraction and formalisation using SVN and SBVR for automated healthcare. In: Proceedings of the 23rd Australasian Conference on Information Systems, pp. 1–11. ACIS (2012)

149. Küng, P., Hagen, C.: The fruits of business process management: an experience report from a Swiss bank. Bus. Process Manag. J. **13**, 477–487 (2007)

150. Bajec, M., Krisper, M.: Issues and challenges in business rule based information systems development. In: Proceedings of ECIS 2005, p. 100 (2005)

151. Levi, K., Arsanjani, A.: A goal-driven approach to enterprise component identification and specification. Commun. ACM **45**, 45–52 (2002)

152. Kumar, R.L., Stylianou, A.C.: A process model for analyzing and managing flexibility in information systems. Eur. J. Inf. Syst. **23**, 151–184 (2014)

153. Embury, S.M., Shao, J.: Analysing the impact of adding integrity constraints to information systems. In: Eder, J., Missikoff, M. (eds.) CAiSE 2003. LNCS, vol. 2681, pp. 175–192. Springer, Heidelberg (2003). https://doi.org/10.1007/3-540-45017-3_14

154. Kovacic, A.: Business renovation: business rules (still) the missing link. Bus. Process Manag. J. **10**, 158–170 (2004)

155. Royce, G.: Integration of a business rules engine to manage frequently changing workflow: a case study of insurance underwriting workflow. In: Proceedings of AMCIS 2007, pp. 495–505. Springer, Heidelberg (2007)

156. Majdalawieh, M., Sahraoui, S., Barkhi, R.: Intra/inter process continuous auditing (IIPCA), integrating CA within an enterprise system environment. Bus. Process Manag. J. **18**, 304–327 (2012)

157. Rudra, A., Yeo, E.: Key issues in achieving data quality and consistency in data warehousing among large organisations in Australia. In: Proceedings of the 32nd Annual Hawaii International Conference on Systems Sciences, pp. 8–23. IEEE (1999)

158. Tan, C., Sia, S.K.: Managing flexibility in outsourcing. J. Assoc. Inf. Syst. **7**, 10 (2006)

159. Moreira, A., Araújo, J., Whittle, J.: Modeling volatile concerns as aspects. In: Dubois, E., Pohl, K. (eds.) CAiSE 2006. LNCS, vol. 4001, pp. 544–558. Springer, Heidelberg (2006). https://doi.org/10.1007/11767138_36

160. Leonardi, M.C., Leite, J.C.S.P.: Using business rules in extreme requirements. In: Pidduck, A.B., Ozsu, M.T., Mylopoulos, J., Woo, C.C. (eds.) CAiSE 2002. LNCS, vol. 2348, pp. 420–435. Springer, Heidelberg (2002). https://doi.org/10.1007/3-540-47961-9_30

161. Jiménez, L.G.: XCM: conceptual modeling for dynamic domains. In: Delcambre, L., Kop, C., Mayr, H.C., Mylopoulos, J., Pastor, O. (eds.) ER 2005. LNCS, vol. 3716, pp. 449–464. Springer, Heidelberg (2005). https://doi.org/10.1007/11568322_29

162. Mahadevan, L., Kettinger, W.J., Paul, R.: A three level model of SOA maturity: toward achieving sense and respond. Presented at the Americas' Conference on Information Systems (2009)

163. Norta, A., Eshuis, R.: Specification and verification of harmonized business-process collaborations. Inf. Syst. Front. **12**, 457–479 (2010)

164. McCarthy, R.V., Claffey, G.F.: Task-technology fit in data warehousing environments: analyzing the factors that affect utilization. J. Int. Technol. Inf. Manag. **14**, 4 (2005)

165. Webber, W., Moffat, A., Zobel, J.: A similarity measure for indefinite rankings. ACM Trans. Inf. Syst. **28**, 1–38 (2010)

166. Dwork, C., Kumar, R., Naor, M., Sivakumar, D.: Rank aggregation methods for the web. In: Proceedings of the 10th International Conference on World Wide Web, pp. 613–622. ACM (2001)

167. Dummett, M.: The Borda count and agenda manipulation. Soc. Choice Welf. **15**, 289–296 (1998)

168. Xiaoyun, C., Yi, C., Xiaoli, Q., Min, Y., Yanshan, H.: PGMCLU: a novel parallel grid-based clustering algorithm for multi-density datasets. In: 1st IEEE Symposium on Web Society, SWS 2009, pp. 166–171 (2009)

169. Chen, L., Li, X., Han, J.: Medrank: discovering influential medical treatments from literature by information network analysis. In: Proceedings of the Twenty-Fourth Australasian Database Conference, vol. 137, pp. 3–12. Australian Computer Society, Inc. (2013)

170. Fagin, R., Kumar, R., Sivakumar, D.: Comparing top k lists. SIAM J. Discret. Math. **17**, 134–160 (2003)

171. Triantaphyllou, E.: Multi-criteria Decision Making Methods: A Comparative Study. Springer, Boston (2013). https://doi.org/10.1007/978-1-4757-3157-6

172. Saaty, T.L.: Decision making with the analytic hierarchy process. Int. J. Serv. Sci. **6**, 83–98 (2008)

173. Hwang, C.-L., Yoon, K.: Multiple Attribute Decision Making: Methods and Applications a State-of-the-Art Survey. Springer, Heidelberg (2012). https://doi.org/10.1007/978-3-642-48318-9

174. Detwarasiti, A., Shachter, R.D.: Influence diagrams for team decision analysis. Decis. Anal. **2**, 207–228 (2005)

175. Lahdelma, R., Salminen, P.: SMAA-2: stochastic multicriteria acceptability analysis for group decision making. Oper. Res. **49**, 444–454 (2001)

176. Groves, R.M., Fowler Jr., F.J., Couper, M.P., Lepkowski, J.M., Singer, E., Tourangeau, R.: Survey Methodology. Wiley, Hoboken (2011)

177. Sarker, S., Lee, A.S.: Does the use of computer-based BPC tools contribute to redesign effectiveness? Insights from a hermeneutic study. IEEE Trans. Eng. Manag. **53**, 130–145 (2006)

178. Strong, D.M., Volkoff, O.: Understanding organization–enterprise system fit: a path to theorizing the information technology artifact. MIS Q. **34**, 731–756 (2010)

179. Eisenhardt, K.M.: Building theories from case study research. Acad. Manag. Rev. **14**, 532–550 (1989)

180. Glaser, B., Strauss, A.: The Discovery of Grounded Theory: Strategies for Qualitative Research. Aldine Publishing Company, Chicago (1967)

181. Pettigrew, A.M.: Longitudinal field research on change: theory and practice. Organ. Sci. **1**, 267–292 (1990)

Printed in the United States
By Bookmasters

Printed in the United States
By Bookmasters